# SHORT Texts, BIG Impact

**35** Strategies for Strengthening Reading and Writing Skills

Kim Carlton, M.Ed.

## Contributors

Kara Ball, M.S.Ed.
Trisha DiFazio, M.A.T.
Jennifer Jump, M.A.
Katie Schrodt, Ph.D.

## Publishing Credits

Corinne Burton, M.A.Ed., *President* and *Publisher*
Aubrie Nielsen, M.S.Ed., *EVP of Content Development*
Kyra Ostendorf, M.Ed., *Publisher, professional books*
Véronique Bos, *Vice President of Creative*
Cathy Hernandez, *Senior Content Manager*
Courtenay Fletcher, *Senior Designer*

## Library of Congress Cataloging-in-Publication Data

Names: Carlton, Kim, author.
Title: Short texts, big impact : 35 strategies for strengthening reading and writing skills / Kim Carlton.
Description: Huntington Beach, CA : Shell Educational Publishing, Inc., [2025] | Includes bibliographical references.
Identifiers: LCCN 2024048818 (print) | LCCN 2024048819 (ebook) | ISBN 9798765929391 (paperback) | ISBN 9798765929407 (ebook)
Subjects: LCSH: Reading comprehension--Problems, exercises, etc. | English language--Composition and exercises. | Learning strategies. | Time management.
Classification: LCC LB1050.45 .C343 2025  (print) | LCC LB1050.45  (ebook) | DDC 372.47--dc23/eng/20240211
LC record available at https://lccn.loc.gov/2024048818
LC ebook record available at https://lccn.loc.gov/2024048819

## Image Credits:

Pages 2, 20, 39, 54, 64, 66, 70, 71, 74, 78, 89, 93, 97, 102 courtesy of the author. Pages 9 and 62 courtesy of Katie Schrodt. Pages 26, 28, and 32 from *Untold Stories* © 2022 Teacher Created Materials. Page 30 from *Focused Reading—Student Guided Practice Book* © 2014 Teacher Created Materials.

---

The classroom teacher may reproduce copies of materials in this book for classroom use only. The reproduction of any part for an entire school or school system is strictly prohibited. No part of this publication may be transmitted, stored, or recorded in any form without written permission from the publisher.

Website addresses included in this book are public domain and may be subject to changes or alterations of content after publication of this product. Shell Education does not take responsibility for the future accuracy or relevance and appropriateness of website addresses included in this book. Please contact the company if you come across any inappropriate or inaccurate website addresses, and they will be corrected in product reprints.

All companies, websites, and products mentioned in this book are registered trademarks of their respective owners or developers and are used in this book strictly for editorial purposes. No commercial claim to their use is made by the author or the publisher.

A division of Teacher Created Materials
5482 Argosy Avenue
Huntington Beach, CA 92649-1039
**www.tcmpub.com/shell-education**
**ISBN 979-8-7659-2939-1**

© 2026 Shell Educational Publishing, Inc.
Printed by: **WAL**
Printed in: **USA**
PO#: **15948**

Teachers come to us in many forms.

This is for all the teachers in my life: the ones who raised me, the ones who shaped me, the ones I taught alongside, and for the ones that will follow.

And in honor of one of my life's teachers in particular: my aunt, Annette Henigan.
Annie, I hope you love this story as much as I do.

# TABLE OF CONTENTS

**INTRODUCTION: SHORT TEXTS, BIG IMPACT** ..................................................... 1
- My Long Journey to the Short Text .......................................................... 2
- The Power of Short Texts .................................................................... 3
- Find Short Texts Everywhere ................................................................ 4
- Why Short Texts Can Have a Big Impact ...................................................... 5
- Who Can Use Short Texts .................................................................... 8
- How to Use These Strategies ............................................................... 10
- A Final Thought on Making a Big Impact .................................................... 10

## PART 1: READING

**USING SHORT TEXTS FOR READING** ............................................................. 13
- Selecting Short Texts ..................................................................... 13
- First Reading of the Text ................................................................. 14
- Reentering the Text (Second Readings and Beyond) .......................................... 14
- Exploring Choices Authors Make ............................................................ 15

**READING STRATEGIES FOR SHORT TEXTS** ....................................................... 16
- Core Reading Strategy #1: Annotation ...................................................... 17
- Core Reading Strategy #2: Zoom In: Analyzing Author's Craft ............................... 19
- Core Reading Strategy #3: Quick Writes .................................................... 21
- Give Me Five .............................................................................. 23
- Layered Annotations: Pronoun Practice ..................................................... 25
- Layered Annotations: Cohesion Connectors .................................................. 29
- Zoom In to Explore Italics ................................................................ 32
- Zoom In to Untangle Syntax ................................................................ 34
- Be Bold ................................................................................... 36
- Word Spokes ............................................................................... 38
- Caption Creator ........................................................................... 39
- Roll a Response ........................................................................... 41
- 3-by-5 .................................................................................... 42
- Evidence Battle ........................................................................... 43
- Potent Quotables .......................................................................... 46

© Shell Education

136447—Short Texts, Big Impact

# PART 2: WRITING

## USING SHORT TEXT FOR WRITING AND REVISING ...... 51
Writing and Learning .................................. 51
The Writing Process .................................. 52
The Role of AI in Writing Instruction .................. 57

## SHORT WRITING AND REVISION STRATEGIES ...... 59
Core Writing Strategy #1: Micro Writing .............. 60
Core Writing Strategy #2: Mentor Texts, Anchor Charts,
    and Writer's Notebooks .......................... 63
Core Writing Strategy #3: Sticky Note Revision ...... 66
The Three-Word Summary Sentence .................. 67
Social Media Thesis .................................. 69
The Six-Word Memoir .................................. 71
Song (Re)writer ...................................... 73
Infographics .......................................... 76
Storyboarding for Prewriting ........................ 78
The Unstuck List ...................................... 81
Expand a Sentence .................................. 84
SCAMPER: One-Word Revision ........................ 86
10% Off Revision ...................................... 88
Roll a Revision ...................................... 90
Cohesion Connectors for Writing .................... 92

# PART 3: FEEDBACK AND ASSESSMENT

## FEEDBACK WITH AN IMPACT ...... 97
Effective Feedback .................................. 98
Motivation and Progress .............................. 99

## SHORT FEEDBACK STRATEGIES .....101

Walk and Talk .....101

Pair and Share .....102

Check and Go .....102

Pile and Grade .....103

The Short Rubric .....104

## APPENDIXES .....107

## REFERENCES .....125

## INDEX .....130

## ABOUT THE AUTHOR .....135

## DIGITAL RESOURCES .....136

# INTRODUCTION: SHORT TEXTS, BIG IMPACT

"Even when you know you should start small, it's easy to start too big."

—James Clear, *Atomic Habits*

I will admit that, despite being a writing teacher, I found writing this book exceptionally hard. I have been teaching and presenting writing strategies for almost two decades, so turning these ideas and strategies into paragraphs and chapters should have been simple. I used to say to my classes, "Just keep the pen moving, and the words will come." But my own blinking cursor mocked me.

I am sorry, former students: I was wrong. Getting the pen moving was hard for me too.

Closing all the tabs in my brain to focus on writing even a single paragraph was surprisingly challenging. At issue: this book was long and deeply intense work. My phone, on the other hand, held an unlimited stream of small posts, quick videos, and short articles. I scrolled through Instagram for a break. I took a fast spin through my news feed to see what was happening in the world. Sending a few quick emails never took long. Ironically, I was surrounded by text: all the ones I was reading and the one big one I was not writing.

Why was this project, one that I loved and was deeply invested in, so hard to complete?

It was the sheer amount of writing I needed to produce that made it hard to start, continue, and finish. I was overwhelmed by my own outline. It was a writer's paradox: Since it felt too hard to finish, it was impossible to start. I felt a new wave of empathy for every student in my class. Every time I opened the file, I found a new error to fix or sentence to correct. This task felt too big; it was hard to even get the pen moving.

Overwhelmed, I called Trisha DiFazio, a friend of mine who recently finished her own first book. She said I needed to break down my big writing goals into smaller ones. Instead of setting

INTRODUCTION

a goal to finish a chapter by the end of the week, I should focus on finishing a small section by lunch. Trisha told me to text her when I finished that chunk. She sent me a goal thermometer I could color in when I completed a section. It was a small act of kindness, and after getting a couple of sections under my belt, I turned a corner. (Thanks again for that push, Trisha.)

> "Everything starts with a sentence. Sentences are mini compositions."
> —Bruce Saddler

Making it all the way through a novel or an essay can be a struggle for any student, even those who enjoy reading and writing. But for students who have never found reading or writing easy or fun, starting the book or writing a paragraph can feel too overwhelming to begin.

We all need someone who can support us when our own self-doubt keeps us from starting. As teachers, we can be that support for our student readers and writers. We can use shorter texts to help them find momentum. We can focus students on writing just a few sentences to get them started. We can break a literacy task down to make it manageable.

## My Long Journey to the Short Text

My favorite English teacher in high school assigned *Bartleby, the Scrivener: A Story of Wall-Street*, a novella by Herman Melville, instead of the much longer *Moby Dick*. *Bartleby* clocks in at about 8,000 words compared with the over 200,000 words dedicated to the big white whale. Mr. Sullivan told us that with so much to read and study in American literature, there was no reason to spend an entire semester suffering through one monster text when we could learn what we needed to know about moody Melville in thirty-two pages.

I loved *Bartleby*. I read every word of that text more than once. Because we read the shorter text, we focused on depth instead of getting lost in breadth. My copy is covered in margin notes. I wrote the best essay of my life about *Bartleby*. I credit that little novella, and Mr. Sullivan, with turning me into an English teacher. I felt like a real scholar that year reading Melville, instead of being the kid who skimmed the CliffsNotes of *Moby Dick* the night before the test.

**I still have the paper!**

But for some reason, the lesson about the power of short texts didn't follow me into my first classroom. I felt that my students needed to experience the *entire* work, which means they suffered through all the acts of *Julius Caesar* and they slogged through every word of the party scene in *The Great Gatsby*. One of my favorite "short" stories took us three days to read aloud in class. By the end, there was little energy or time for analysis or discussion. My students were bored and disengaged before we started exploring the text's deeper meaning. We didn't have time to analyze the impact of a word or sentence because we were focused on what was happening in the text and who the characters were. Not to mention how hard it was helping absent students catch up.

Trying to get my reluctant readers and writers to make it through the long texts I assigned wasn't really working for any of us. Even in the days before smartphones, it was a challenge to convince students to pick up the pen and write anything, much less an entire essay. The same was true when asking students to read a chapter on their own. They might start strong, but within a few minutes, seven kids had asked for the bathroom pass, two had put their heads down, and one was making paper footballs to flick at his friends.

Like many teaching innovations, teaching with short texts happened because my original plan hit a roadblock. In my case, the copy machine was down. I was only able to project a small section of text, and I found my students were more focused and our conversations were richer than when we were all looking at our own copies of a multi-page story. We had more time for rich analysis because we weren't battling to finish the text.

I started increasing the use of smaller reading and writing tasks. We worked to write and revise a great thesis statement. We did a close read of two paragraphs of a text to analyze the author's craft. The smaller texts and tasks were more manageable. I developed lists of ten-minute lessons, and we checked them off as we accomplished them.

Now, don't misunderstand me: I loved sharing longer texts with students. There is no other way to get to the gut-punch endings of *Where the Red Fern Grows* or *Charlotte's Web*. I still get teary reading the final line of *To Kill a Mockingbird*. There was always room for both short and long texts in my classroom.

## The Power of Short Texts

When I talk about the power of short reading and short writing, I am referring to the idea that using short texts allows time for instruction and practice. Skills like analyzing an author's craft and inference are often not tackled on a first read. If we are spending days plodding through the text to get to the place where we can ask big questions, students are not getting enough practice with those skills. In my own classes, I used to spend forty minutes reading the text with students, and then we would rush through analysis during the last ten minutes.

In a blog post for the National Council of Teachers of English (NCTE), Julie Wright (2020) describes how starting with reading short texts on a topic can lead to longer texts as students find their interest piqued. Short texts, she explains, "feel manageable…they give the reader a sense of *I can read this from beginning to end*" (para. 8). Short texts also use "every inch of real estate on the page to get the information or point across" (para. 10), making them perfect for teaching and instruction. The economy of words means every word counts and carries meaning. There is a teachable moment hiding in almost every sentence. And because it takes less time to read, using a short text leaves lots of time for practice, discussion, and feedback.

A short text gives us space for teaching big concepts and practicing challenging skills. Nancy Frey and Douglas Fisher say that, for close readings, short texts are better because the work is so time-consuming (2013). With shorter texts, we can lower the cognitive load and save space for learning. Shorter writing tasks help students focus on improving the content or practicing a revision strategy instead of reaching a word or page count. Reading and writing small is still reading and writing. It honors the complexity of these skills.

## Find Short Texts Everywhere

We are surrounded by a sea of text, but that text keeps evolving as new forms of communication, social media, and technology evolve. Students are reading and writing more than we think, but it is likely in the form of captions, memes, posts, and text messages. As we prepare students for the future, we should also be preparing them to read and write texts of all kinds, including short, succinct texts.

To write short texts actually takes great skill. You have to distill your thoughts into key ideas, with precise word choice, clear syntax, and thoughtful transitions. According to Jim VandeHei, Mike Allen, and Roy Schwartz, cofounders of Axios and authors of *Smart Brevity* (2022), we are surrounded by a "fog of words" (12). The solution is writing that is "short, but not shallow" (15). VandeHei, Allen, and Schwartz promote the power of "saying a lot more with a lot less" (12).

But it is not just journalists who are advocating for shorter texts to write and read. Frey and Fisher have long advocated for using "short, worthy passages…because close readings can be time consuming" (2013, 46) They note that these texts can be "news articles, poems, or short stories" as well as "short passages from longer texts, especially when a section is especially challenging" (47).

Doug Lemov and his coauthors recommend close reading bursts, which focus on a discussion of just one or two sentences of text. These close reading bursts can be planned or unplanned but showcase the "power of learning more by doing a little bit of something every day" (Lemov, Driggs, and Woolway 2016, 109).

Even when a text is short, we may not spend much time reading it. According to VandeHei, Allen, and Schwartz, eye-tracking studies show we spend twenty-six seconds, on average, reading a piece of text. Our brain decides in seventeen milliseconds if we like a link we have clicked on. In the amount of time it took to type this sentence, you may have already zoned out, checked your phone, or skimmed ahead (VandeHei, Allen, and Schwartz 2022).

> **FAMOUS SHORT TEXTS**
>
> Preamble to the Constitution = 52 words
> Emily Dickinson's "Because I could not stop for Death" = 127 words
> George Washington's Second Inaugural Address = 135 words
> Maya Angelou's "Phenomenal Woman" = 258 Words
> The Gettysburg Address = 272 words
> Lou Gehrig's Farewell Speech = 277 words
> Kurt Vonnegut's "Harrison Bergeron" = 1095 words
> The Declaration of Independence = 1320 words

This book doesn't aim to tackle the impact of too much time on our phones or whether reading books on paper or on a screen is better for comprehension. Instead, I am focused on strategies teachers can use to help students dive deeply into reading comprehension and writing skills, to evaluate the impact of a word or phrase, to find and apply author's craft, and to get more practice and feedback on those skills. Reading and writing shorter texts gives us instructional time to focus on building confident readers and writers.

Well-crafted short texts, from billboards to social media, are plentiful, creating opportunities for more frequent engagement with reading and writing. By the time students become teenagers, most of the text they engage with will be short: captions, videos, and text messages. It makes sense to help young people navigate the reading and writing that surround them so they can consume and produce short texts with clarity and critical thinking.

## Why Short Texts Can Have a Big Impact

From a purely practical standpoint, short texts leave more time for practice, discussion, and reflection. Spending three days reading an entire "short" story leaves little space for learning. We spend more time getting through it than we do talking about it. According to Mike Schmoker, "Our curriculum must be liberally infused with frequent opportunities for students to read, discuss, argue, and write about what they are learning" (2018, 28).

> **EVERYDAY SHORT TEXTS**
> - Social media posts
> - Photo captions
> - TikToks
> - Memes
> - Signs and billboards
> - Songs
> - Text messages
> - Emojis (Yeah, I said it!)

### Lessen the Cognitive Load

Brain research has consistently shown that short-term, or working, memory is limited by time and space (McLeod 2023). The number of things we can retain in our working memory is called *cognitive load*. Like any heavy load that you carry, you might be able to hold onto it for a little while, but eventually, you have to set it down.

The same is true with learning. "When our working memory is overloaded, learning is minimal" (Hattie and Clarke 2019, 84). When students are weighed down trying to decode words or remember details from earlier in a passage, they have less cognitive space for other tasks. They may even run out of space. If the cognitive load of a text is too heavy, there is little space for the working memory to determine the main idea or grapple with a text feature.

Working with shorter texts can lessen the cognitive load for students. There are fewer details to manage, fewer names to keep track of, and fewer plot points to remember. John Hattie and Shirley Clarke emphasize that awareness of cognitive load is important when designing instruction: "We should avoid overloading students with additional activities that don't directly contribute to learning" (2019, 85). They recommend "break[ing] learning into parts that can be linked," which is the beginning of "deep understanding" (2019, 85).

### Provide Access to Challenging Texts

For students struggling with reading fluency, grade-level texts may feel out of reach for instruction. But the instinct to provide easier texts doesn't pay off in learning dividends. In "The Challenge of Challenging Text," Timothy Shanahan, Douglas Fisher, and Nancy Frey acknowledge that working with a complex text is, well, complex: "Teachers may be tempted to try to make it easier for students by avoiding difficult texts. The problem is, easier work is less likely to make readers stronger" (2012, 62). For students striving to read complex, grade-level texts, shorter versions of those texts can give students practice that feels possible.

Providing all students access to complex, grade-level texts is critical. Students benefit from reading a text even if it requires more of an instructional lift. According to The New Teacher Project (TNTP), "Students spent more than 500 hours per school year on assignments that weren't appropriate for their grade and with instruction that didn't ask enough of them—the

## INTRODUCTION

equivalent of six months of wasted class time" (2018, 4). However, "in classrooms where students had greater access to grade-appropriate assignments, students gained nearly two months of additional learning compared to their peers" (5).

Working with a more complex text requires careful planning and scaffolding. According to Frey and Fisher, "If students are going to access complex texts, they must be given the time to read and reread, to respond to questions that encourage them to return to the text, and to discuss their ideas in the company of others" (2013, 15). Shanahan writes, "The idea of teaching with more complex text aims to expand the role of teaching to maximize the amount of student learning" (2020b, para. 25).

A rich text in a smaller form means students still engage with the complex text without the task itself overwhelming students. By keeping the complex text short, we have time and space for teaching and supporting students. We can provide important vocabulary, build up content knowledge, and untangle complicated syntax bit by bit.

---

### NAVIGATING COMPLEX TEXTS

All students deserve access to rich, powerful, challenging text. Engaging students with texts of grade-level complexity should spark their curiosity and garner interest. Complex texts build students' knowledge and vocabulary, equipping them to comprehend increasingly challenging material. Exposure to complex texts allows students to grapple with rich content, deepens their understanding, and promotes critical thinking. Access to complex texts requires ensuring students have the right tools in their toolboxes to tackle them.

Complex text doesn't have to be long. Excellent shorter text selections feel more manageable to students, while still providing practice with the skills needed to navigate challenging vocabulary, syntax, and text structures. Consider chunking, or breaking, texts into smaller, manageable sections. This provides students with access and opportunities to engage meaningfully with challenging material without overwhelming them. We often think that every word of a text is essential, but sometimes, a specific section holds the crux of a text's meaning and is most valuable for students to focus on. Purposefully breaking text into smaller sections allows students to dive deeper and find meaning in a few powerful lines, making longer texts more accessible and impactful.

—Jennifer Jump, coauthor of the *What the Science of Reading Says* series

---

### Provide More Frequent Feedback

John Hattie's synthesis of research on effective classroom practices has consistently shown that frequent and actionable feedback has a "powerful impact on student learning" (Fisher, Frey, and Hattie 2016, 32). But not all feedback is created equal. To have the most impact, feedback should be specific, actionable, and timely. In *Flash Feedback*, Matthew Johnson writes, "It makes a lot of sense that regular feedback given shortly after a task is completed would have a larger impact than intermittent feedback received weeks later" (2020, 12).

Learning activities with short texts and short writing allow for more frequent and targeted opportunities for feedback. We don't have to wait until we get to the end of the book or chapter. Ideally, students should receive meaningful feedback every day instead of waiting for the teacher to grade, record, and return assignments days, or even weeks, later. Receiving feedback on an essay weeks after it was written doesn't help students become better, more confident writers. However, when students write and revise a few sentences, the teacher can give feedback in the teaching moment or during the next class session.

You can learn more about ways to provide brief feedback in part 3.

## Create Small Wins

There's another benefit to shorter reading and writing tasks: Students see the progress they are making much more quickly. The idea that they will become better readers and writers by the end of the school year is hard for students to see in October. Having students compare writing at the beginning and end of the year is great, but why wait until June to see what all the hard work was for?

Teresa Amabile and Steven Kramer studied employees to understand what brings joy and engagement at work. They found that "of all the things that can boost emotions, motivation, and perceptions during a workday, the single most important is making progress in meaningful work" (Amabile and Kramer 2011, para. 3). Though students are not employees, no one would argue that school and learning are not *work*.

If we think of a classroom like a workplace, teachers are similar to managers seeking to motivate workers. Students are motivated when they feel like they are making progress. Mike Gaskell writes, "Incremental victories, or small wins . . . can give a much-needed boost to students' confidence and motivation" (2021, para. 1). He explains, "Data presented toward progress can encourage even the most reluctant learners to improve" (para. 9). Students' small wins can create a self-reinforcing progress loop where one step toward a goal leads to motivation and drive to keep working to the next step.

Imagine these two scenarios and think about which teacher is supporting students step-by-step.

> **Scenario 1:** *Class, remember that your final persuasive essays are due next week. They need to have a works cited page and at least four pieces of evidence.*

> **Scenario 2:** *Yesterday, we crafted and revised your claim statements for your persuasive essays. If I didn't meet with you one-on-one yesterday, I left you a few notes on your exit tickets. Today, we will work to find one great piece of evidence to support that claim and learn how we can embed it into our writing.*

In the second scenario, each small step of the assignment has a checkpoint for feedback. It is progress toward a larger goal. The monster task of writing a persuasive essay is split apart and practiced in smaller sections. Questions and concerns are addressed early, before moving onto the next step.

At the end of the day, who doesn't like crossing everything off a to-do list? Making that little checkmark on each task makes it easier to move on to the next one.

INTRODUCTION

> ## SHORTER TEXTS AND SEL
>
> Shorter texts support students' social-emotional learning (SEL) by reducing the cognitive load, making it easier to concentrate on both comprehension and emotional connection. When reading feels less overwhelming, students are more likely to engage with the content and experience a sense of accomplishment and confidence. This is particularly beneficial for reluctant and/or struggling readers, as the shorter format allows them to experience success without the stress posed by longer, more complex text selections. By working with content that they can fully grasp, students experience frequent moments of success, which fuels motivation and engagement. Identity has a significant impact on student behavior and learning. These small wins are crucial in shaping students' perceptions of themselves as capable and confident learners.
>
> —Trisha DiFazio, coauthor of *Social-Emotional Learning Starts with Us*

## Who Can Use Short Texts

Reading and writing instruction should not be isolated to the language arts classroom. Students read in every content area, and writing is a tool to help them understand those texts better. According to Steve Graham and Michael Hebert, "Writing about science, math, and other types of information promotes students' learning of the material" (2010, 6). Tim Shanahan writes, "We should be teaching students how to use writing in concert with reading to improve comprehension, increase knowledge and to conquer academia" (2020a, para. 21).

Asking students to read and produce short texts can be a useful approach for teachers who don't think of themselves as language arts teachers. You don't have to spend days working with a novel to build up readers. Students don't have to write multi-paragraph essays to become more confident writers. There often isn't time to teach both content and corresponding literacy skills. But incorporating quick strategies to help students comprehend short pieces of reading and produce short bursts of writing can have a big impact on helping students better understand the content.

> ## SHORT TEXTS FOR YOUNG LEARNERS
>
> Young children are highly capable writers when provided appropriate support and scaffolding. While writing demands a complex balance of ideas, transcription, phonics, and phonemic awareness skills, several high-impact practices help develop confident young writers:

# INTRODUCTION

- Through *explicit modeling*, teachers demonstrate the writing process in real time, thinking aloud to show how writers generate ideas, organize thoughts, and sound out words.

- *Picture book mentor texts* serve as short, effective writing models for young children to collaboratively study for genre-specific ideas and craft moves (see "Teaching Writing with Mentor Texts in Kindergarten" by Schrodt et al. 2021). *Oral storytelling* and *oral rehearsal* build narrative skills and vocabulary before writing begins, reducing the cognitive load of facing a blank page. With partners, students practice orally telling stories in specific genres, working through organization and craft ideas, and rehearsing sentences.

- Students also rehearse steps in the writing process through practiced *self-talk* (see "Supporting Emergent Writing with Oral Storytelling Strategies" by Schrodt, FitzPatrick, and McClain 2023).

- *Drawing* serves as a crucial planning tool, allowing children to visualize and add details to their stories without the burden of transcription. *Studying and producing illustrations* can help bolster children's narrative development (see "An Exploration of the Impact of Quality Illustrations in Children's Picture Books on Preschool Student Narrative Ability" by Davis, Schrodt, and Lee 2024). *Adding labels* to drawings bridges the gap between pictorial and written expression.

- Through *shared writing experiences*, teachers and students collaboratively compose text, modeling genre-specific elements and mechanics while supporting developing writers.

- *Regular reflection, specific feedback*, and picture-supported *writing checklists* help young writers develop metacognitive skills.

These scaffolds, combined with *growth mindset* development through literature like *Your Fantastic Elastic Brain* by JoAnn Deak, *positive self-talk* ("Writing is hard, and I can do hard things!"), and encouragement of "*brave spelling*," create an environment where children see themselves as capable writers who can focus on expressing ideas without fear of perfect spelling (see "Becoming Brave Spellers" by Schrodt, Fitzpatrick, and Elleman 2020).

—Katie Schrodt, associate professor, Middle Tennessee State University

## How to Use These Strategies

This book is divided into two main sections: short reading strategies and short writing strategies. In addition to descriptions of the strategies, I have included some ideas to help make them your own.

- Teacher Talk is a sample script or think-aloud to share with students.
- Teaching Tips are based on lessons learned in the trenches, when students misunderstood or became confused about what we were learning.
- Make It Happen with Any Text gives support for selecting texts to do this work.
- Make It Happen at Any Level shows you how the strategy looks across different grade bands or with different groups of students.
- Make It Better has extension ideas and next steps.
- Make a Big Impact shows how the strategy accomplishes a bigger literacy goal.

I also included some text pairings and short texts that you might use in your classroom to try these strategies out. As you're reading through a strategy, be sure to turn the page, as many strategies continue on the next page.

When I taught, I mixed these strategies in the same class day. We would read a short bit of text, talk about what it meant and how it was structured, and then write a little bit. Some days there was more reading and some days there was more writing, but I always tried to include both.

As students completed these short reading and writing opportunities, I used the time to walk around and lean over the shoulder of every student at least once a day to provide informal feedback. Sometimes it was a conversation, sometimes it was a thumbs-up stamp, sometimes it was just a nod. I made notes on my clipboard to remind me which students I needed to circle back to and spend more time with tomorrow. Not every day was perfect. Not every day was even good. Pep rallies, fire drills, afternoon malaise, and spring field trips got in the way. But every day was about making a little progress toward the big goal: creating confident readers and writers.

The strategies in this book can be mixed and matched, combined and modified, shared, and transformed to meet your instructional goals, your students' needs, and the demands of the text you are working with. Each one is about ending the day by getting a small win. And who couldn't use more of those?

## A Final Thought on Making a Big Impact

Teaching is hard. Sometimes we are the ones who need the win. When I could see that students used something I taught them right away, we all got to celebrate. When we made it through a hard text together as a class, we all got a gold star for the day. No matter how hard I tried, I couldn't fix every need my students had. But I could help students grow just a little stronger as readers and a little more confident as writers each day.

My former students are now professors, entrepreneurs, engineers, screenwriters, teachers, and so much more.

That was my big impact.

# PART 1: READING

# USING SHORT TEXTS FOR READING

A short text provides opportunities to practice multiple reading skills and makes that practice easier to approach. In an era full of teaching challenges, getting students to turn the page and pick up the pen can be a first win. While the goal of this section is to show how the strategies can be used with short texts, they can be used with texts of any length.

## Selecting Short Texts

A short text can be a section of a longer text, a short article, a headline, an infographic, or even a visual. I have used billboards, text messages, monologues from movies, letters to the editor, sudden fiction, and six-word memoirs to teach everything from inference and evidence to figurative language and research skills.

I often used a short section of a longer work to think about big ideas and practice important skills. One of the best teacher feelings is when a student wants to read more than what you share in class. According to Wright, "Short texts invite interested readers to read more" (2020, para. 9). Sometimes I handed out the whole text but had students focus on just a portion. Other times, I provided the text as an excerpt.

Even classic literature can use a little condensing from time to time. If you studied Shakespeare's *Julius Caesar* in high school, you may remember Mark Antony's "friends, Romans, countrymen" speech.

### A BRIEF WORD ABOUT READING ENTIRE BOOKS

Reading short texts or excerpts does not replace reading full novels or student-selected independent reading. Both long and short texts are important to the literacy life of students. Recent studies show that the number of books students are reading for pleasure has dropped substantially over the last generation (U.S. Department of Education 2024).

Classrooms can strike a balance between short, instructional jaunts of reading and writing to build skills and stamina, and the rich joy of finishing a self-selected chapter book or novel. There is space for both. When we start a workout regimen, we don't start by running marathons. Working with shorter texts for both reading and writing provides a foundation for independent reading and builds the stamina needed for reading longer texts in and out of the classroom.

But you've likely long forgotten the drawn-out battle scenes in Acts IV and V. (If you forgot there even was a battle in *Julius Caesar*, no shame!) With limited instructional time, and a long list of important skills students needed to master, I often provided a quick summary of a section of text that didn't have an instructional pay-off. I would rather spend that extra time going deeper into the work that matters.

## First Reading of the Text

It is difficult, if not impossible, for students to analyze a text accurately without first having a general overview of what the text is about. More than skimming or previewing the text, a first read prepares students for what's to come.

With any text, we want to introduce key terminology and activate background knowledge. The Science of Reading calls our attention to these components. Louisa Moats emphasizes the importance of activating and building background knowledge: "Everything we comprehend through listening is filtered through the lens of what we already know and believe" (2020, 217). We know that students who have a wide vocabulary and deep background knowledge on a topic will have an easier time comprehending text. We also know that reading widely helps build the very background knowledge and vocabulary needed to read more complex texts.

### WAYS TO DO A FIRST READ

- Modeled read-aloud by the teacher
- Paired reading
- Silent/independent reading
- Playing an audio recording

Many of the strategies in this section are conducted *after* a first reading of the text. Teachers may opt to conduct that first read in a variety of ways: a teacher-modeled read-aloud for the whole class, a paired reading where partners take turns, an independent silent read, a recording or audiobook, or some combination of these.

## Reentering the Text (Second Readings and Beyond)

I like to use the phrase "reentering the text" instead of "rereading." Many students have a misconception of rereading as something you only do when you are not a strong reader. When asked to reread, students will often go back to the first word of the first line, instead of digging into the sections where comprehension breaks down. Kelly Gallagher refers to "second draft reading," or helping students learn that "meaning can be found beyond the surface layer of the text" (2004, 82). Lemov, Driggs, and Woolway use the term *layered reading,* the idea that students reread the text "strategically to engage it in different ways that make a difference" (2016, 64). Each of these terms suggests that we gain more when we return to the text a second or third time. They also honor the deep work of comprehension that often follows a basic understanding or first read of the text.

We can reenter the text multiple times, looking for different things with each reading. Nancy Frey and Douglas Fisher explain that incorporating repeated readings "requires that students have expanding purposes" (2013, 47). Since we have already done our first read, we are returning to the text to uncover more meaning. When we return, we don't always start with the first word. We can hop to a specific section or ask students where they would like to reenter the text. We can move directly to the main idea or a section that is dense and tangled with complex syntax and vocabulary.

# Exploring Choices Authors Make

Reading and writing are inextricably linked. When we read, we think about the author's meaning and intent. When we write, we are working to share meaning with others. To read a text critically, we have to think beyond the words on the page and notice the moves that an author makes to impact the reader.

Author's craft encompasses a wide variety of choices that authors make when writing. Everything from the details that are included and the way the text is structured to the use of a specific word or punctuation mark reflects a decision that an author made deliberately. According to Lester Laminack in *Cracking Open the Author's Craft: Teaching the Art of Writing*, "Craft is an intentional use of techniques…to create a desired impact upon the reader and to evoke a response from the reader" (2016, 17).

As a reader, examining the intentional choices an author made can be part of comprehending the text. By closely reading a text, looking at the author's craft, we can better understand why the text was written and how it is structured. Penny Kittle notes, "You will open a window into how reading and writing are intimately connected, both in teaching and learning. When we intentionally connect them [reading and writing] in our teaching, we strengthen students' abilities in both" (2022, 13).

Examining an author's craft is both a reading and writing strategy. When students see an author's choices as intentional, they are more likely to consider the small moves they get to make as writers. Katie Wood Ray calls these "crafted places" or "those places where writers do particular things with words that go beyond just choosing the ones they need to get the meaning across" (1999, 28).

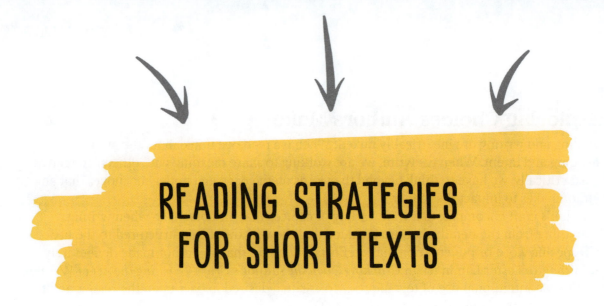

"We accomplish more when we focus on less."
—Mike Schmoker, *Focus* (2018)

This chapter begins with three core reading strategies that I employed in my classroom year-round for a variety of purposes. After I taught these instructional routines, we returned to them often. Students knew what to do and felt comfortable enough to use the routines without lengthy directions. Depending on the text, my students, the objective, and the time I had available, I modified and adjusted these strategies. They can be used for quick dips into a text or for longer lessons.

The first several times we used a strategy, I provided extensive modeling and guidance. But I always had an eye on gradual release to student-focused work, with the goal being student independence and automaticity.

Following the core strategies is a collection of reading and author's craft strategies that are perfect for working with any short text. These strategies can be combined with others and paired with the writing strategies in part 2 to practice a range of literacy skills during a single lesson, for a class period, or throughout a class day.

# READING STRATEGIES FOR SHORT TEXTS

## Core Reading Strategy #1: Annotation

Annotation is a tried-and-true method for deepening understanding of text. Mike Schmoker calls annotating a kind of teacher-modeled think-aloud. "Through frequent modeling of reading, underlining, and annotating…we can accelerate the attainment of core intellectual skills by several years," leaving students "ready to practice [critical reading] themselves alone, then in pairs—with our guidance" (2018, 105).

Active readers connect to background knowledge, decode words, encode meaning, grapple with syntax, visualize images, and synthesize elements simultaneously when reading a text. Reading and annotating requires even more multitasking from a reader. This is especially true for striving readers still developing their skills and when students are reading challenging texts for the first time.

> **SKILLS AND TOPICS FOR ANNOTATION LAYERS**
>
> - Summarizing chunks or paragraphs
> - Identifying and distinguishing people (names, pronouns, groups)
> - Locating key events or steps
> - Identifying evidence and reasons
> - Locating figurative language
> - Tracing motifs and symbols
> - Connecting cause to effect

To support these readers, I explicitly teach annotation in layers, focusing on one thing at a time. Kelly Gallagher calls this *first- and second-draft reading* (2004). Annotations can be done on any text for any purpose. Perhaps students need to trace the events in the text to show chronology. Perhaps they need to link causes and effects. Students don't need to annotate a text in its entirety if only some sections prove tricky. The key is working in layers: Readers should look for one thing at a time, returning to the text for a new purpose and using new annotation markings each time.

The general process is the same each time so students will become comfortable with the task. We want them to build automaticity with the act of reading and reentering the text in layers. You can change the annotation task based on the demands of the text or the skill of the moment (e.g., plot, figurative language, persuasive elements). I have done annotations to look at techniques as broad as organization and as narrow as pronoun usage.

1. Decide what sections of the text warrant further study. Perhaps it is the most important bit of the text or an especially complicated section. Not every word or sentence needs to be annotated. Consider what would help students unpack the meaning of that section.

2. Provide students with a copy of the text with numbered paragraphs, or have students number the paragraphs before beginning. This allows the class to navigate the text quickly.

3. Have students give the text an initial read. You may opt to read the text aloud or have students read silently.

4. Take a few moments to have students jot down their initial thoughts and reactions. Ask questions such as these:

   - What is the text mainly about?
   - What is the main idea?

© Shell Education

136447—Short Texts, Big Impact    **17**

# READING STRATEGIES FOR SHORT TEXTS

- What questions or wonderings do you have?
- Where did you get confused in the reading?

5. Direct students to the section of text you plan to dig into further.

6. Use a projector to display the text on the board and model annotation. I like to use colored pencils for this work so the annotations stand out.

*Teacher Talk:* *I know this section of the text has lots of characters and their names all sound similar. It is hard to keep the characters straight in my head, and that can be confusing. I am going to reenter this text with my colored pencils and mark the things done by Duncan in red so I can see them easily.*

*In this section, I see that Duncan is standing outside of the room looking in through a window. I am going to underline that in red. That means he is only able to see and hear part of what is going on. I think I am going to write a note out to the side to remember that Duncan doesn't know the full story.*

*Next, I see that Duncan rushes in and offers to help. I am going to underline that in red too. It shows that he is helpful and kind. I think I will make a note of that on the side.*

7. After quickly modeling, turn the projector off and invite students to reenter their own copies of the text to continue looking for a specific technique or element.

If you model too much, students will simply copy your markings. While it can be satisfying to see all their beautiful papers that match your own, this doesn't help students with the challenging work of reading.

8. Allow students time and space to annotate a section of the text. They can work in pairs as needed. Larger groups are not as effective for this task.

9. Bring the class back together to discuss the annotations. Ask students what they marked and why they marked it. It is not critical that every student marks everything the same way.

10. Add the next layer of annotations. I like to use a different color or notation to help show each thing we are annotating.

*Teacher Talk:* *This section of the text was confusing when we first read it because it could be hard to tell what each character was doing and thinking in the scene. We started by underlining all the things Duncan did in red. Now, let's enter the text looking for the things Everest did in this section. I am going to underline them in blue so I can compare where Everest is in this section too.*

Repeat steps 5 to 8 for each layer of annotations. Students will often speed up on successive layers as they become more comfortable with the task and the text.

You can continue to use the same text for other annotations based on student needs and the demands of the text. Each annotation happens in a separate layer—one thing at a time—with discussion and reflection between the rounds.

**18**  136447—Short Texts, Big Impact

© Shell Education

# Core Reading Strategy #2:
# Zoom In: Analyzing Author's Craft

"It is my practice to try to understand how valuable something is by trying to imagine myself without it."

—Herb Kelleher, cofounder and former CEO of Southwest Airlines

The Zoom In reading strategy is used to spotlight, examine, and consider specific sections of a text and analyze the choices a writer has made. In addition to supporting students' comprehension of the text and its author's purpose, this strategy can extend into writing. As students learn about how author choices convey meaning, they can explore the impact of making those same choices in their own writing.

This is similar to zooming in on a digital image to look more closely at the details. This core reading strategy and the questions to ask are the same no matter the grade level of students, the text you are using, or the skill you are teaching.

1. Have students read the text in its entirety. Use whatever method makes sense for your group. Remember, it is hard to explain the impact of something if you haven't read the text.

2. "Zoom in" to a section of text for a closer look. The selection of text can be an entire paragraph, a sentence, or even just a specific word. The choice can be teacher-directed, teacher-nudged, or student-directed. Ask the following questions:

   - What is the author doing in this section?
   - Why is the author doing it?
   - How can you use this technique in your own writing?

3. Consider creating an anchor chart and adding each author's craft technique the class identifies to the chart. (See appendix B for sample anchor charts.)

The Zoom In questions in step 2 are intentionally designed and scaffolded, and they don't change. Analyzing author's craft helps students better understand the texts in their hands and connect the insights they gain to their own efforts as authors.

## Analyzing Author's Craft

- **What is the author doing in this section?**
- **Why is the author doing it?**
- **How can you use this in your own writing?**

**What is the author doing in this section?** The first question helps students identify and name a technique the author is using, which makes it easier to spot when another author uses it in a different text. The question also ensures that students are on the same page, examining the same technique. In some cases, students can name the literacy device, strategy, or technique based on prior learning. Other times, they might recognize that *something* is happening but don't yet have the academic language for it. One time, a student called italics "drunk letters." Another student referred to an adjective as an "adnoun." Both students were making important connections with their invented terms. Naming the techniques authors use helps students with future close readings and even "empower[s] students to try out the strategies in their own writing" (Bogard and McMackin 2015, 41).

**Why is the author doing it?** The second question speaks to the impact of the author's technique on the reader. Katie Wood Ray says it is not about guessing what was in the writer's head, but rather about "what we see in an author's text for *ourselves*" as readers (1999, 125). She suggests it is helpful to have students think about the author's *other* options in crafting that part of the text, helping students see that writing is a "process of decision making" (1999, 43). I also like to use a similar prompt: What would change if the technique weren't there?

**How can you use this in your own writing?** The final question moves students' analysis from a reading comprehension strategy into their writing practice. As Penny Kittle says, "Reading and writing are and have always been united. When we intentionally connect them in our teaching, we strengthen students' abilities in both" (2022, 13).

After students think about the choices an author has made, they can apply that strategy to their own writing. Laminack writes, "By thinking about the reasons for decisions and the intentions behind them, we begin to discover the ways we can use the same crafting techniques ourselves" (2016, 23). Doug Lemov and colleagues talk about the synergy between reading and writing and explain that students who "examine choices carefully…develop the range of grammatical or stylistic structures they can use [and] are most aware of the connection between stylistic choices and authorial intent" (2016, 161).

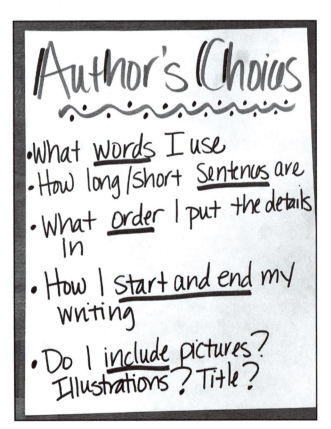

But be prepared, teacher friends: After the first time you Zoom In to examine an author's crafted use of italics or an onomatopoeia, everything your students write for the rest of the year will use that new technique. This means they saw a technique a writer used to convey meaning, and they can now use it themselves. Celebrate that. It is a good day of teaching.

# Core Reading Strategy #3: Quick Writes

Writing a response to a text is not a new technique. I think we can all recall writing a book report at some time in our school careers. (And I bet some of us had to read it aloud while in costume!) Ample research supports writing as a pathway to learning as it "improves a student's ability to recall information, make connections between different concepts, and synthesize information in new ways" (Terada 2021, para. 5). Schmoker points out that "any form of writing, short or long, generates and refines thought" (2018, 106).

The quick write is a simple way to provide processing time, pace instruction, and assess student learning. Students respond to some element of a text in quick bursts of writing, usually two to three minutes.

I love when the reason behind a classroom practice is explained in a resource that has little to do with education directly. In the 2018 bestseller *Atomic Habits*, James Clear talks about the "Two-Minute Rule" for starting a new habit. The idea, he says, "is to make your habits as easy as possible to start" (163). Much like the Two-Minute Rule of creating new habits, a two-minute quick write is a gateway to more writing. Clear says, "You can't improve a habit that doesn't exist," and the same is true for reading and writing (2018, 167). Students can't get better if they don't get started. Two minutes is the perfect start time for writing. "The secret is to always stay below the point where it feels like work" (165).

> As students respond in short bursts of writing to prompts, questions, and texts, they build literacy routines.

Quick writes build good reading and writing habits. As students respond in short bursts of writing to prompts, questions, and texts, they build literacy routines. Slowing down reading to respond and process at what Robert Marzano calls "strategic stopping points" leads to dramatic increases in "students' understanding of new information across content areas and at every grade level" (2009, 87). But quick writes provide more than just places to stop and catch your breath. Schmoker emphasizes how these moments are foundational to student learning: "If we want all students to learn, they need frequent opportunities to write and share their thoughts with partners" (2018, 98).

Just like starting any habit, creating time and space for writing as a response to reading can be a challenge. Miriam Plotinsky, author of *Small but Mighty: How Everyday Habits Add Up to More Manageable and Confident Teaching*, explains that subtle changes to classroom practices can yield big results. She notes, "Teachers must intentionally identify and develop incremental habits for themselves and their students" (Plotinsky 2024, para. 7). Using what James Clear's *Atomic Habits* (2018) calls "habit stacking," teachers can add quick writes to an existing daily routine. Start with adding a quick write at the beginning or end of the literacy block (or at the beginning or end of the class period). Once students grow comfortable with the process, expand it by adding quick writes after students read a short text or a single paragraph. This small habit of using bursts of writing to process big ideas and dense texts helps students read more complex texts and write responses to them. "Even the tiniest moves toward creating a stronger foundation for success yield some immediate benefits" (Plotinsky 2024, para. 21).

Perhaps the most flexible of the core strategies, quick writes can be done anytime: at the

READING STRATEGIES FOR SHORT TEXTS

start of the literacy block or class period, before reading, during reading, after reading, before discussion, or at the end of the time period. They can be planned or unplanned. Sometimes you need two or three minutes to set up the next lesson, talk privately with a student, or distribute materials. Often those minutes are lost instructional time. But with a quick write, those minutes can be used to give students space for processing or to collect their thoughts for discussion.

> Quick writes can be done anytime: at the start of the literacy block or class period, before reading, during reading, after reading, before discussion, or at the end of the time period.

I have used quick writes to have students pose their own questions or predictions; we return to them later to see if questions were answered or predictions were right. Quick writes also serve as an ideal launching spot for paired and class discussion. Since everyone comes to the conversation with something to share, it's easy to get started. Below is the process I recommend.

1. Have small paper ready for writing. I like to use a standard 3x3 sticky note or interactive writer's notebooks.

2. Provide students with a just-in-time prompt related to what they are reading. The prompt can ask a specific question about the text, providing a place for students to summarize and process a small chunk of information or ask questions and make connections.

3. Scaffold students' responses as needed. Consider using a sentence frame or word bank. As with all scaffolds, remove it once students become more confident writers.

4. Ask students to take two minutes to write. My colleague Valerie Davenport calls this "No Talking, No Walking" time, since often students see this quiet moment as a perfect opportunity to wander to the trash can, bathroom, pencil sharpener, or any place where they don't have to write.

5. If you are not modeling your own quick write, walk around the room, looking over students' shoulders at their writing. Try to lay your eyes on every student's work every day, even if it is just for a moment. Are students struggling to get started? Are they on the right track? Do they have the materials they need to be successful? Do they have a thoughtful response? A new way of thinking?

6. Ask students to bring their writing to a close. I sometimes ask them to put their writing instruments down when they are ready. I don't like to abruptly call "time," but instead allow every student to finish their thought.

7. Provide time for students to share their responses in some manner. Depending on the lesson, the day, and the time, I might have them share with a neighbor, share with someone in an assigned small group, or share with the whole group. I often ask students whose work I saw if they would be willing to share their "great response."

I like using sticky notes for this work for a couple of reasons. First, sticky notes are a visual cue that this is not formal writing. The focus is on the content, not the mechanics. Second, with this kind of writing, there is no need for a full sheet of paper. Some students become overwhelmed by an entire blank page, and the sticky note is manageable. Finally, a sticky note can be put right back into the text you were studying after you have written it. I have collected enough sheets of paper from under desks at the end of the day to know that if it doesn't have a place to live, writing tends to get thrown away.

See part 3 for ideas for quickly scoring quick writes.

# Give Me Five

Give Me Five is a strategy to support students with identifying the main idea and summarizing after reading a text. Students are given a challenge: Identify the five most important words or phrases in the text. This strategy works since it is a relatively easy lift for most students. All they need to do is mark five words in the text. The challenge comes in determining *which* five words are best.

Collaborative and layered, this strategy ensures that students will use a variety of skills: rereading, synthesizing, and evaluating. As students discuss and debate their choices, they return to the text and the main idea. The final five words are less important than the discussion and debate around why some words are better than others.

1. Have students complete a first read of the text.

2. Ask students to identify the five most important words from the text. Emphasize that they must select exactly five words—no more and no less. Students can highlight, circle, or box the words, or write them on sticky notes.

> **Teaching Tip** Students may ask if compound words, hyphenated words, or contractions count as single words. This shows they are thinking and weighing their words carefully, as well as growing their understanding of grammar concepts. Provide a grammar mini-lesson and decide as a class if such words should be counted as one or two words.

3. Have students pair, share, and compare their lists of words. Each pair should work together to create an agreed-upon list of the five best words.

4. Expand the groups by having pairs join together. The larger groups now refine their lists by coming to consensus about the five best words. You can continue expanding the groups and having each group of students work together to create their list.

5. Return to full-class discussion to determine the best five words for the class. The first two to three words are typically common across groups, but there is often lively debate over the final words. Allow students to debate and defend their choices.

## Make It Better

Students can use their five words to create a one-sentence summary of the text. This sentence can serve as a simple exit ticket or an assessment of learning.

## Make It Happen at Any Level

| Emerging Readers and Writers (K–2) | Multilingual Learners |
| --- | --- |
| Consider asking students for the most important word from a shared text. Have students share their words with the class and then vote on which word is the best. | Use the five most important words to create a word wall for speaking and writing activities related to the text. |

# Layered Annotations: Pronoun Practice

Annotating for annotating's sake could be a tedious timewaster. It is important to design annotation tasks around a text's specific complexities. What makes this text difficult for students to access? Where are they likely to get confused? With those answers in mind, you can design annotations to untangle the tricky spots of a text.

> The examples shown here use the text "What's Right at All Costs" (see page 108 for the full text).

This example of annotating focuses on an area that often causes confusion in a text: pronouns, specifically, when a text contains two individuals who use the same pronoun. Writers use pronouns to add variety to sentences and eliminate repetition, but pronouns can be confusing for readers. Part of what makes pronouns tricky is that the "reader must integrate [the] information from one sentence to the next" (Moats 2020, 241). If the reader isn't clear who "he" is referring to, they can quickly lose the thread of the text.

In texts with more than one individual, dueling pronouns can make it difficult to determine who did what, especially for students developing English proficiency. "One reason that pronouns are particularly difficult is that the referent can only be established by knowing the speaker and context" (Foursha-Stevenson et. al. 2024, 481). In other words, students who are struggling to follow the content of the text will struggle even more to follow it when pronouns are added to the mix.

> "A poor reader's misconception may hinge on something as basic as identifying the referent for a pronoun."
> —Louisa Moats (2020, 242)

For this example, the text is the story of two people, one who helps the other. Students may struggle to identify which details belong to which person. Through annotation, students untangle the two people and better understand the text itself.

1. Have students complete a first read of the text.
2. Ask students to reenter the text and draw boxes around the references to people in the text. Use a think-aloud and model this on one paragraph.

**Teaching Tip** Do not say "names." If you do, students will simply scan for words with initial capitals and think they are done. Instead, I intentionally keep it broad. "People" allows students to consider more than just names. People can be referenced by pronouns, collective nouns, titles, and even country names.

READING STRATEGIES FOR SHORT TEXTS

3. As you model, show students how to draw arrows or lines to connect the names of the people in the text to the other words that are used to identify them. Moats calls these "referential relationships" (2020).

*Teacher Talk:* *So, this first paragraph is about Jose Arturo Castellanos Contreras. The author calls him a "hero" and uses the pronoun "he."*

When tracing the people in the text, students may discover that they need additional annotations to differentiate between separate individuals in the text. Encourage students to brainstorm how they might do that. For examples, students might opt to use different colors, one for each person, or mark them with wavy and straight lines, or add initials or a number above the box.

*Teacher Talk:* *I also noticed that this paragraph mentions more people than only Jose Arturo Castellanos Contreras. I am going to put those people in different colors so I can tell them apart.*

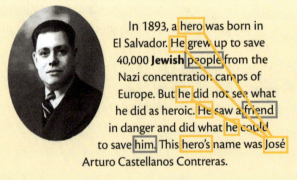

# READING STRATEGIES FOR SHORT TEXTS

4. Turn the task over to students to annotate specific paragraphs or the rest of the text. Allow for conversation and comparison in pairs and trios. In this example, students would also discover that groups of people, organizations, or even countries might be performing the actions of people. This leads to great discussion between students!

5. Compare and share as a class. Students don't need to all mark the same words; what is important is that they think about what text refers to what people.

## Make It Better

In my class, I used a handful of annotations consistently. I tried to use the same codes for those annotations. For example, we drew arrows from causes to effects and put boxes around references to people. I knew it was working when we read new texts and students began putting boxes around people's names and pronouns without any prompting.

## Make It Happen at Any Level

| Emerging Readers and Writers (K–2) | Multilingual Learners |
| --- | --- |
| Emerging readers are being introduced to pronouns. Use a short text or portion of a longer text to emphasize why authors use pronouns. | Work with students to brainstorm a list of ways an author names people in a text. In the example, we see pronouns, collective nouns, names of countries, and names of groups all functioning as actors in the text. Discuss which of these are singular and which are plural and how that affects the verb choice. |

## Make a Big Impact

Pronouns are an especially potent place to see how a text is held together. When students are familiar with the process, they can use it on their own writing to check whether they are using pronouns correctly.

> As the English language evolves, so do our rules of usage. Many publishers and style guides now recognize the use of singular *they* to refer to a person of unspecified gender. For example, according to the Modern Language Association (MLA), the use of singular *they* is no longer considered an error in grammar but has "emerged as a tool for making language more inclusive" (2021, para. 5).

© Shell Education

READING STRATEGIES FOR SHORT TEXTS

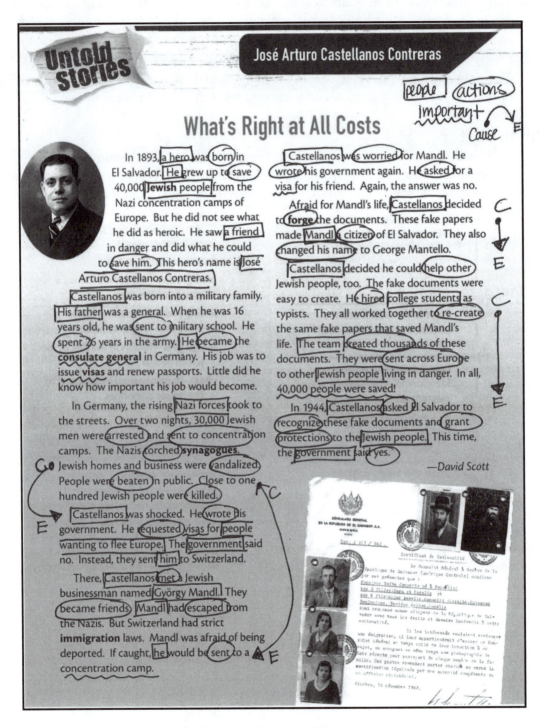

Example of annotated text

READING STRATEGIES FOR SHORT TEXTS

# Layered Annotations: Cohesion Connectors

When readers struggle with the meaning of a text, it is often because they cannot follow the storyline, the narrative flow, or the central idea. Though a reader may be able to make it through the text at a surface level (e.g., read all of the words), not seeing connections between sentences and paragraphs makes it impossible to make inferences, draw conclusions, or read critically.

By using a mentor text as a model, you can help students see the concrete ways authors craft cohesive texts, as well as give students a fix-up strategy for their own reading. Annotating a text with cohesion connectors helps students trace the thread between sentences and paragraphs, and ideas.

> The examples shown here use the text "The Mystery of the Beeswax Wreck" (see page 109 for the full text).

When working with cohesion connectors, consider in advance which words or phrases to use, based on the text. I look for language or ideas that might confuse or slow down readers. Louisa Moats notes that to make meaning, readers need to be able to hold "the previous phrases or sentences(s) in mind while new information is processed, and long or complex passages may exceed a student's processing 'bandwidth'" (2020, 242). Moats recommends activities and practice at the micro level, so students can better understand a text at the macro level.

1. Have students complete a first read of the text.

   *Teacher Talk: Authors connect ideas in a text by tying together words, sentences, and paragraphs and making links between old information and new information. This is called* cohesion. *Authors use a variety of techniques to create cohesion in their writing. By following the threads, you can better understand a text from beginning to end. We will be looking at how the author of this text created a thread that runs through the text.*

2. Start with a detail in the title or opening paragraphs. In this example, the text is about a shipwreck that has been missing for over 200 years. The text is heavy with dates and locations.

   *Teacher Talk: I am going to start with the title and opening lines. The title is "The Mystery of the Beeswax Wreck" and the first sentences say, "Ahh, ancient galleons, shipwrecks, and buried treasure! Stories of adventure in the high seas are irresistible." I am going to put a box around the word "shipwrecks" since it seems to be important and explains what kind of wreck we are going to be talking about. The second sentence includes the phrase "high seas," which is where ships sail. I will put a box around that phrase too.*

3. Draw a line connecting these ideas. This line shows how authors connect ideas from one sentence to another.

© Shell Education

136447—Short Texts, Big Impact  **29**

# READING STRATEGIES FOR SHORT TEXTS

> Ahh, ancient galleons, shipwrecks, and buried treasure! Stories of adventure in the high seas are irresistible. They are especially exciting when they are true. This is the case with a ship that sank off the coast of Manzanita, Oregon. People have been debating its origins for over 200 years.

4. Continue into the next sentence, connecting ideas. Each time the author connects ideas, box the words or phrases and draw a line to link them.

*Teacher Talk:* I see the phrase "a ship that sank," which is a wordier way of saying shipwreck. I also see the author uses the word "its" to refer to that shipwreck. Every sentence in the text is connected to something before it.

> Ahh, ancient galleons, shipwrecks, and buried treasure! Stories of adventure in the high seas are irresistible. They are especially exciting when they are true. This is the case with a ship that sank off the coast of Manzanita, Oregon. People have been debating its origins for over 200 years.

5. Move through the rest of the text carefully, modeling making connections. You will notice connections between sentences and between paragraphs. You may also notice that the author introduces new ideas. In this text, we start to see information about the time period. Use a different color to connect the ideas focusing on details that move the reader through time.

6. When students are ready, have them do this work in small groups. They may see that they have lines from the beginning to the end of the text. If you wish, have them return to the top and use a different color to start a new thread.

> Ahh, ancient galleons, shipwrecks, and buried treasure! Stories of adventure in the high seas are irresistible. They are especially exciting when they are true. This is the case with a ship that sank off the coast of Manzanita, Oregon. People have been debating its origins for over 200 years.
>
> The oldest chapter of this mysterious shipwreck story surfaced in the journal of a fur trader. In 1813, Alexander Henry wrote that a group of Clatsop Indians arrived at the trading post with blocks of beeswax. This

READING STRATEGIES FOR SHORT TEXTS

7. Reflect on the cohesion connections students have made. Ask, "What do you notice about how the author has organized the text?" (*Every paragraph is connected in some way.*) Ask, "What techniques do authors use to create cohesion in their writing?" (*repetition, synonyms, prepositions, and so on*) Consider creating an anchor chart showing ways authors create cohesion.

## Make It Better

It is important to take a moment to pull the lens back and look at the text as a whole. The annotated text should look messy. It's a good mess! This is typical for annotations of cohesive writing. Cohesion is not simply connections between the words at the start of each paragraph. Cohesion reflects intentional connections between the words, phrases, sentences, and paragraphs of a text.

Don't worry if students don't all have the exact same connections. Let students grapple with and debate about where ideas are connected. There should be circles and lines in different colors all over their texts.

## Make It Happen with Any Text

It's easiest to start this practice by using a text that includes some elements of a chronological structure.

## Make It Happen at Any Level

### Emerging Readers and Writers (K–2)

Younger readers might need more modeling to connect ideas. You may also choose to provide examples on an anchor chart before asking students to make their connections. For example, explain that dates and sequence words can be a way authors create cohesion in a sequential or chronological text, then ask them to return to their pieces looking for that example.

### Multilingual Learners

Take a few moments prior to starting this lesson to provide a concrete example of things that are connected and intertwined. You can make a web by tossing a ball of yarn and asking students to hold a piece as it zigs and zags in the room. Demonstrate how tugging on one part of the web moves the whole thing.

This visual metaphor helps students see that sentences and paragraphs they write should be connected. If one part isn't connected, the entire web falls apart.

### Experienced Readers and Writers (6–12)

More sophisticated texts have more sophisticated cohesion connectors. Push students to find connectors beyond simply repetition or dates. Conjunctions are a powerful way to connect ideas. Authors may also use synonyms, antonyms, and demonstrative pronouns such as "this" and "that."

To demonstrate the power of cohesion connectors, have students trace each thread in a different color.

© Shell Education

READING STRATEGIES FOR SHORT TEXTS

# Zoom In to Explore Italics

Authors impact meaning with the smallest of choices. Think about the difference between these three statements: "Please call." "Please call!" and "Please call?" Changing the punctuation changes how a text is read and how it is understood. The same is true for words that are italicized or bolded.

Consider the example "I didn't say he stole the money" from a guide to English by Ann Cook (2000, 25). Cook shows how the meaning of the sentence changes based on the words emphasized: "I didn't *say* he stole the money" and "I didn't say he stole the *money*" have different meanings. In fact, this sentence can have at least seven different meanings just by changing the word that is emphasized or italicized.

> The examples shown here use the text "Ever American" (see page 110 for the full text).

Zooming in allows you to focus students' attention on the small decisions an author makes—in this case, an italicized word—and how they impact the meaning. Using rich mentor texts will allow students to analyze such choices and consider the "intentional touches" authors use "to create a desired impact…and to evoke a response from the reader" (Laminack 2016, 16–17).

1. After a first read of the text, invite students to zoom in for a closer look at a sentence where an author is making a decision that impacts meaning. In "Ever American," the author italicizes the word "normal" in the second paragraph.

> Essa had always lived in America. Yet it seemed to her that she was not a *normal* American. She learned this from school, books, and TV. Americans portrayed there did not look like her family. They did not pray like her or eat the foods she ate. Most of those Americans only spoke English.

2. Ask, "What is the author doing here?" (*italicizing the word* normal)

3. Ask, "Why is the author doing it?" (*The author is emphasizing that what Essa sees as* normal *does not include her own experiences. It also emphasizes that* normal *doesn't mean the same thing to everyone.*)

**Teaching Tip** If students are struggling, try asking the question in another way: "What would change if the author didn't italicize the word?" (*It would seem like there was only one way to be a normal American.*)

**32** 136447—Short Texts, Big Impact

© Shell Education

4. Pull the "zoom" lens back out and ask students to consider why an author would choose to italicize a word. Ask:

- How do italics and bold text convey meaning?
- Why should we pay close attention to them as readers?
- How can we use italics or bold text for impact in our own writing?

## Make It Happen at Any Level

| Emerging Readers and Writers (K–2) | Experienced Readers and Writers (6–12) |
|---|---|
| Compare sentences ending with periods versus question marks versus exclamation marks. Have students act out the sentence as it is read using different end punctuation.<br><br>Example: Puppies. Puppies? Puppies! | Encourage students to find examples of sentences where the punctuation changes the entire meaning of the sentence, often with humorous results.<br><br>Example: "Let's eat, Grandma" versus "Let's eat Grandma." |

READING STRATEGIES FOR SHORT TEXTS

# Zoom In to Untangle Syntax

This strategy allows you to zoom in to look at syntax or sentence structure. In *What the Science of Reading Says About Reading Comprehension and Content Knowledge,* Jennifer Jump and Kathleen Kopp point out that "more complex sentences place higher comprehension demands on students" (2023, 109). According to Louisa Moats, close reading with explicit focus on how ideas are connected helps increase comprehension (2020).

> The examples shown here use the text "What's Right at All Costs" (see page 108 for the full text).

By using a sentence that needs to be untangled, you can give students an opportunity to explore how sentences and syntax work to create meaning. When zooming in at the sentence level, I like to look for either a sentence that is incredibly dense (that is, a sentence that has lots of phrases and clauses that need to be untangled) or a turning-point sentence that impacts the overall understanding.

1. Complete a first read of the text with students.

2. Invite students to zoom in for a closer look at a specific sentence in the text. For this example, I am zooming in on the following sentence: "Afraid for Mandl's life, Castellanos decided to forge the documents."

3. Ask students to identify the subject and predicate of the sentence. You can simplify this by having them identify the subject and verb of the sentence.

| Zoom In: *"Afraid for Mandl's life, Castellanos decided to forge the documents."* | |
| --- | --- |
| **Subject** | **Predicate** |
| *Castellanos* | *decided to forge the documents* |

Tell students that when this sentence is untangled, we see a main sentence, or independent clause, and an additional phrase: *Afraid for Mandl's life.* Have students cover the independent clause, revealing only the remaining phrase. Ask students if this phrase changes the meaning of the main sentence.

| Zoom In: *"Afraid for Mandl's life, Castellanos decided to forge the documents."* | |
| --- | --- |
| **Phrase** | **Sentence/Independent Clause** |
| *Afraid for Mandl's life,* | *Castellanos decided to forge the documents.* |

## READING STRATEGIES FOR SHORT TEXTS

5. Sometimes it is helpful to explore the impact of a phrase by asking students to consider what they lose if it is gone. Ask students to cover up the phrase *Afraid for Mandl's life.* Then ask, "So, could we take this portion out of the sentence entirely since it isn't part of the independent clause?" (*No! It adds critical information!*) Ask students, "How does the meaning of the sentence change when the phrase is added?" (*With it, Castellanos is a hero for wanting to save his friend's life. Without it, Castellanos simply committed a crime for no reason.*)

6. After examining the impact of a single phrase on a sentence's meaning, discuss why it is important for readers and writers to untangle twisted sentences.

## Make It Happen with Any Text

Find a sentence where changing a phrase changes the meaning of the sentence. Rewrite the sentence and ask students to zoom in and look at the impact of the change. What changed when you changed the wording? Why was the original wording important?

## Make It Happen at Any Level

| Emerging Readers and Writers (K–2) | Experienced Readers and Writers (6–12) |
|---|---|
| Have students practice adding a single adjective to a simple sentence. How does it change the meaning?<br><br>For example:<br><br>Revise this sentence by adding a single word: *The dog buried his head and ignored the knock at the door.*<br><br>*The **sleepy** dog buried his head and ignored the knock at the door.*<br><br>Answer: Adding the adjective "sleepy" may explain why the dog didn't go to the door. He was too tired to move! | Have students practice finding different kinds of phrases in texts and explaining their impact. Encourage students to find prepositional phrases, appositive phrases, or gerund phrases. |

© Shell Education

136447—Short Texts, Big Impact **35**

# Be Bold

Be Bold aims to support several skills—summarizing, vocabulary development, and sentence construction—at the same time. Using a short text with a few vocabulary words that are in bold font, students create a single sentence under specific constraints and within the reading context. According to Louisa Moats, "Words are most likely to be 'owned' if they are learned with a network of related ideas" (Moats 2020, 234). Using the bold-font vocabulary words to write a one-sentence summary accomplishes both reading and vocabulary goals with minimal preparation or planning.

This is more effective than having students look the word up in the dictionary; research has shown that to be an ineffective use of instructional time with a negligible impact on word knowledge (Allen 1999). Having students write sentences with vocabulary words also leaves much to be desired. Janet Allen says this practice "has little apparent impact on word knowledge and language use" (1999, 2).

Writing summaries is one of my favorite activities because of how versatile it is. Writing a one-sentence summary of a shared text means all students have the same starting point. When students share and compare, they can focus less on the content and more on how their peers constructed their summaries. Adding pre-selected vocabulary keeps this activity challenging but within reach while giving students meaningful interactions with new vocabulary.

1. Have students complete a first read of a short text that includes words in bold font.

2. Challenge students to write a one-sentence summary of the text using all the words in bold font.

3. Have students share and compare their sentences.

4. As students share, discuss the different ways they incorporated the bold words and formed sentences.

    - Point out when a student changed the tense of a verb or modified its part of speech.
    - Spotlight how some students used a conjunction to make a sentence work or used a prepositional phrase to include all the words and ideas.

*Teacher Talk: I noticed how one student took the bold adjective* competitive *and made it into the verb* compete. *I see how another student took the bold noun* victory *and turned it into the adjective* victorious. *Lots of words can be used in different ways if we change the suffix to change the part of speech.*

## Make It Better

If the text doesn't have bold words, have students pick the words that they think should be bold. For more information, see Give Me Five on page 23.

## Make It Happen with Any Text

Choose a short text with a few bold vocabulary words. You can use this strategy anytime you have a few extra minutes to work with a text.

## Make It Happen at Any Level

| Multilingual Learners | Emerging Readers and Writers (K–2) |
|---|---|
| Support students in learning new vocabulary with examples of how the bold word may be used in different ways.<br><br>For example, the word *attempt* can be a noun or a verb. It can be changed to *attempting* or *attempted* by adding a suffix. | Allow students to write the sentence using only some of the selected words.<br><br>Students might also craft a two-sentence summary. Utilize sharing and comparing time as an opportunity to combine those two sentences into a single sentence using conjunctions or other revision strategies. |

# Word Spokes

Word Spokes (Rasinski et al. 2011) are an effective way to help students uncover the meaning of a common Latin or Greek root and apply it when reading unfamiliar words. Studying a root increases word knowledge of not just a single word but an entire family of words. Students improve their understanding of both known and unknown words containing the root.

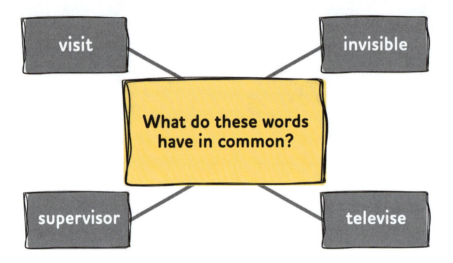

1. Identify a word or words from the text. This example, based on the text "What's Right at All Costs" (page 108), uses the word *visa*. It is connected to the Latin *vis-* meaning "to see."
2. Display four words that use the same base.
3. Ask, "What do these words have in common?" (*They all contain* vis–.) "What connects the meaning of all the words?" (*They all have to do with seeing or watching*.)
4. Have students brainstorm and share other words that include the Latin *vis–*. (For example, students may offer words like *visor, visitation, indivisible, revise,* and *visual,* among others.)
5. Have students return to the text to find how the author uses the Latin root in the text. In this example, it is in the sentence: *His job was to issue visas and renew passports.* Ask students, "How does what we know about the Latin root *vis–* connect to the word *visa*?" (*A visa is a visible stamp that allows you to go to another country on a visit.*)

### Make It Happen with Any Text
Since "more than 90 percent of [English] words with more than one syllable…are derived from Greek or Latin," you can find words for analysis within the pages of nearly any text (Rasinski et al. 2020, 19).

# Caption Creator

Graphic elements in texts support comprehension by adding or clarifying information. Informational texts often have more visual content, and that content can be critical to understanding the text. "Visual texts help us locate directions using a map, make choices based on advertisements, and simplify and summarize critical information in graphs and charts" (Cappello and Walker 2020, 20).

With a high number of informational and multimodal texts in curricular materials, students need direct instruction in reading graphics and connecting information from them to the main text. "Teachers [should] seize every opportunity to comment explicitly on the value of graphics in constructing meaning from text and to model extracting and constructing meaning from graphics" (Roberts et al. 2013, 7).

To prepare students for this activity, and to support informational text reading, spend time pointing out and examining the graphics and captions that accompany a variety of texts. Over a few days, students will likely encounter photographs, maps, tables, charts, images of documents, illustrations, and comics in texts across the content areas. Introduce and discuss the kinds of information provided in captions for these graphics. Create an anchor chart and add examples to it.

1. Choose an informational text that includes one or more descriptive graphics with captions. Conceal or remove the captions, if possible.
2. Have students read the text.
3. Ask students to write a caption to accompany the image.

**Teaching Tip** Point students to the anchor chart for inspiration and ideas.

4. Have students share their captions with the class. After sharing, have students compare their captions to the author's. How are they alike? How are they different?
5. Ask, "In what ways do captions help us understand a text? How are graphics and visuals important to a text?"

## Make It Happen at Any Level

| Emerging Readers and Writers (K–2) | Experienced Readers and Writers (6–12) |
| --- | --- |
| Instead of hiding the entire caption, black out only specific words and have students guess what information is missing. | Provide a text without any graphics. Ask students to find or create an image that goes with the text and craft a caption for it. |

## Make a Big Impact

The brevity of captions means they include only information that is critical to understanding an image. This mini summary supports comprehension and puts a spotlight on how text features like visuals, graphics, and captions add to the text. By practicing writing captions, students test their summarizing skills and increase their knowledge of how the caption's text works to convey meaning.

# Roll a Response

Roll a Response is a low-stakes way to get students engaged with and talking about a text. This student-centered activity can be done quickly as a replacement for traditional study questions, or it can be extended into longer written responses that include text evidence supporting answers.

1. Have students read an informational text.
2. Place students in groups of four. Provide each group with one number cube and a *Roll a Response* activity sheet (page 121).
3. Have students roll the cube to determine the question they will need to answer about the text.
4. Students can all write responses to the same question, or each roll to answer a different question. Students share their responses orally or in writing with their small groups.

## Make It Better

Extend this activity by asking all students who rolled a particular number to form a group and craft a response as a team. Ask students to write their responses on sticky notes before sharing and then collaborate with other students who had the same number.

## Make It Happen with Any Text

Modify the questions to match the text, genre, or current skill focus. I find it useful to review the state reading standards and create a question to match each key standard.

For literary texts, students might be asked to discuss character changes, plot, or theme. For poems, they might be asked to look at the rhyme scheme or use of figurative language.

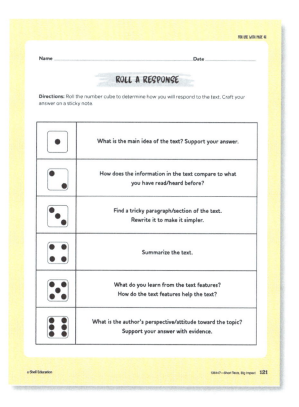

# 3-by-5

Sometimes I have big plans for a text—maybe we will use it as part of a larger text set, as a quick read for building some background knowledge, or for a writing activity. Other times, I need to quickly assess how students are applying reading skills on their own. In both instances, I want to engage students with a reading activity that is easy to create and grade and that can be expanded or compressed based on the time I have available. This strategy is the answer.

The 3-by-5 strategy is, quite simply, a play on words. Students are asked to provide three main points from the reading in five minutes or less. And as the name implies, they write their responses on a 3 x 5 index card. Bigger and sturdier than a sticky note, the lined 3 x 5 index card is a nonthreatening entry into writing and response. The small amount of space keeps writing focused, and note cards are easy to collect and assess as needed.

Key details are an ideal place to start, since, as Frey and Fisher note, "understanding this information should be critical to understanding the text" (2013, 55). Starting with the three most important key details can also help "scaffold students' understanding as they respond to more complex questions" (Frey and Fisher 2013, 55).

This strategy is easy to set up, and the discussions that follow can effectively extend learning.

1. After reading a short text, give each student a lined 3 x 5 index card.

2. Ask students to write what they consider to be the three main points from the text.

3. Set a timer for five minutes.

4. When time is up, there are a variety of ways to extend the learning.

   - Use a "Give One and Get One" protocol, where students share and collect additional key points from their peers.
   - Have students work in groups to share and compare their key points and create a single list of the best three key points (similar to Give Me Five on page 23).
   - Collect the index cards as exit tickets and use them for assessment.

## Make It Better

Have students add summary sketches to the back of the 3 x 5 cards, creating personalized summary postcards.

## Make It Happen at Any Level

| Multilingual Learners | Experienced Readers and Writers (6–12) |
| --- | --- |
| Support learners by segmenting the text into three parts and ask students to come up with the key point from each section. | Revise the instructions to ask students to pose three discussion questions or three quiz questions for the class based on the reading. |

# Evidence Battle

Many states have standards and assessments asking students to respond to questions about the text and to support those answers with relevant or well-chosen text evidence. Formulas like ACE (Answer-Cite-Explain) or ATE (Answer-Text-Explain) help students understand the structure and organization of a response but do little to help students select the best text evidence.

Finding text evidence is easy. Students can simply choose almost any sentence in a text and copy it as their answer. Finding the right text evidence is much harder. Students need to be taught how to choose the *best* or most relevant text evidence to answer the question. This requires students to compare and evaluate text options to determine which best supports the answer. This higher-order thinking takes time and intentional, explicit instruction.

## Problems with Text Evidence

- **The answer is wrong.**

- **The evidence isn't the strongest example in the text.**

- **The evidence needs paraphrasing or context.**

- **The evidence doesn't connect to the answer the student has written.**

In *The Paradox of Choice*, Barry Schwartz says that having too many options makes it harder to choose (2016). Too many options can overload our brains and paralyze us, keeping us from deciding anything. Looking at an entire text, even a short one, provides countless options for textual support, making it difficult for students' brains to make the best choice.

Evidence Battle focuses squarely on the process of evaluating text evidence based on four options.

1. Select a text. You can use any genre of text, but I find informational or opinion/argumentative texts to be a little easier to use with students.

2. Have the class complete a first read of the text.

3. Pose an open-ended question. (See page 119 for text-dependent writing prompts.)

4. For example: *After reading "What's Right at All Costs," how would you describe José Arturo Castellanos Contreras? Support your answer with evidence from the text.*

5. As a class, brainstorm answers to the question. Work together to determine the best answer. For the text "What's Right at All Costs," the class might brainstorm these adjectives to describe Contreras: *brave, compassionate, dedicated*, and *a good friend*. After a discussion, the class might decide on *brave* as the class answer.

# READING STRATEGIES FOR SHORT TEXTS

> **Teaching Tip** There can be more than one answer to the question, but coming to a single class answer is critical in the "battle" for the best evidence.

6. Ask students to reenter the text and find the best piece of evidence from the text to support the answer. In this example, we are looking for evidence to support the answer that Contreras can best be described as *brave*.

7. Students write their best text evidence on a sticky note.

8. Move students into groups of four. Have them number off, from 1 to 4, so each student has a number. (See page 123 for an Evidence Battle template.)

9. Working in rounds, students "battle" their text evidence. In each round, two pieces of text evidence face off in a battle for dominance.

   Round 1: Call for students 1 and 2 to battle for the best text support. Students 3 and 4 debate which of the two pieces of text is the winner and why.

   Round 2: Reverse the roles. Call for students 3 and 4 to battle for the best text support. Students 1 and 2 debate which of the two pieces of text is the winner and why.

   Round 3: The winners from rounds 1 and 2 compete for the best text evidence. The group determines the champion text evidence for the table.

   Round 4: Bring all the groups back together to have the evidence-battle champions face off against each other. When finished, crown the class champion of text evidence.

10. Ask students to integrate the winning text evidence into their original responses.

> Use any short text with a text-based writing prompt. You can find a list of possible prompts on page 119. The example here uses the text "What's Right at All Costs" (see page 108 for the full text).

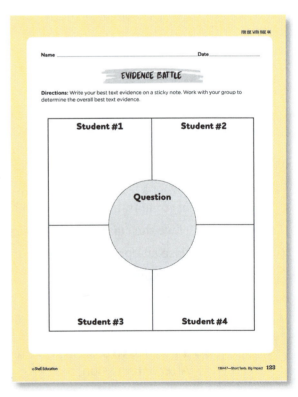

The battles and debates can be a little loud and rambunctious, but that is part of the charm of this activity. I like to use a timer for the rounds to keep things moving. It is important to point out after all the battling that sometimes the first or most obvious piece of evidence might not be the best piece of evidence. When you have two or more options to consider, you often wind up with a better answer.

## Make It Better

There are hidden mini-lessons and teachable moments living in this activity. Consider teaching students the difference between a direct quote and a paraphrase, how to punctuate with quotation marks, how to cite evidence, or even how to weave textual support into an existing sentence.

## Make It Happen at Any Level

| Emerging Readers and Writers (K–2) | Experienced Readers and Writers (6–12) |
|---|---|
| Challenge students with *This or That*. Provide two pieces of text evidence and ask: "Which is better evidence—this one or that one?" Have students vote for the best answer. | Have students write out their textual support with proper citations and an explanation to bring to battle. This gives students practice in providing context and explanations for their textual support. |

READING STRATEGIES FOR SHORT TEXTS

# Potent Quotables

Think quickly: How many inspirational quotes do you have hanging in your classroom? If you are like me, the answer is no fewer than five. I was a sucker for a poster with a quippy life lesson printed over a gauzy nature backdrop. In addition to supplying poster content, such quotes fill our social media feeds and phone photo apps.

Famous quotes are the ultimate short text—powerful, well-crafted, and pointed. But there is often mystery around how these quotes became famous. Though we may have been called on to memorize and recite famous quotes from literature and history in school, rarely did we dissect what the speaker or author was doing stylistically that made a quote famous. My favorite English teacher, Mr. Sullivan (remember him from the introduction?), shared a world of quotes with us, and made us analyze *why* they were memorable. This activity aims to do the same: to not only break down a memorable quote for meaning, but to also analyze how it is written.

Though examining longer texts for examples of author's craft can be difficult, playing with famous quotes is often easier because of their length.

1. Post a favorite famous quote. For example:

   > "If you have built castles in the air, your work need not be lost; that is where they should be. Now put the foundations under them."
   >
   > —Henry David Thoreau, *Walden*

> **Teaching Tip** Always double and triple check that the quote is real and came from the actual person to whom it is attributed! The internet is packed with inaccurate or fake quotes by everyone from Mark Twain to Maya Angelou.

2. Give students an opportunity to respond to the content of the quote. They can't analyze the author's craft if they don't know what the author is saying! You may need to provide historical context to the discussion—famous quotes weren't written or spoken in isolation.

3. Tell students that authors make purposeful choices about words, sentence structure, and punctuation to achieve maximum impact. Famous quotes are often famous for a reason—they share an inspirational idea using simple, yet often elegant wording that sounds good when said aloud.

4. Work with students to pinpoint what choices the author made that led to the quote becoming famous. In the example by Thoreau, we might talk about the words *castles* or *foundations*.

5. Ask students, "How would the quote be different if we changed those words?" (*"Castles" sound big and fancy. If he had written "houses" instead, it wouldn't sound as important. Since this is a quote about setting and achieving goals, it makes sense to use the bigger, grander "castles" for the goal instead of the much simpler "houses."*)

**46** 136447—Short Texts, Big Impact

© Shell Education

6. You might collect some of these insights into a list or anchor chart of choices authors make for maximum impact. An example anchor chart is on page 112.

### A Short List of Favorites

"There is always light, if only we're brave enough to see it. If only we're brave enough to be it."

—Amanda Gorman

"The opposite of love is not hate, it's indifference. The opposite of art is not ugliness, it's indifference. The opposite of faith is not heresy, it's indifference. And the opposite of life is not death, it's indifference."

—Elie Wiesel

"One child, one teacher, one pen, and one book can change the world."

—Malala Yousafzai

## Make This Happen with Any Text

Famous quotations go hand in hand with social studies curriculum, but there are also many quotes that apply to science content. If you are departmentalized, social studies and science teachers can pair with ELA teachers to develop cross-curricular lessons.

## Make It Happen at Any Level

| Multilingual Readers | Experienced Readers and Writers (6–12) |
| --- | --- |
| Some sound techniques (alliteration, rhyme, assonance, etc.) are lost when a quote is translated into another language. Discuss with students the concept that how a quote works in one language may be quite different from how it works in another. | Have students find their own favorite quotes to bring in, share, respond to, and analyze. Explain to students that high-stakes writing tasks as well as college and scholarship essays often start with a famous quotation as a prompt. This type of analysis helps them prepare for such tasks. |

# PART 2: WRITING

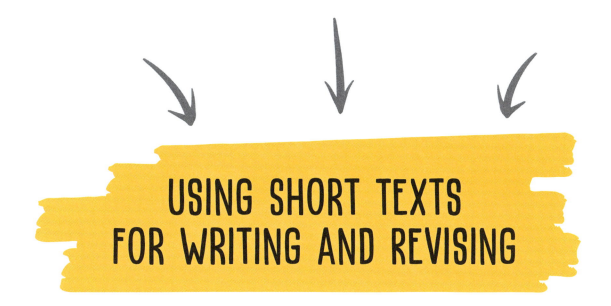

# USING SHORT TEXTS FOR WRITING AND REVISING

Writing is hard for students. It takes lots of time. The rules of writing are complicated and not always consistent. And since writing is a personal expression, feedback can feel harsh.

Teaching writing is hard for teachers too. There is never enough time to teach writing in a literacy block. I made valiant efforts to include writing during the school day, often in the form of journal entries at the start of class. I displayed a slide with a prompt each day of the school year. I used a lot of clip art and Comic Sans font on my slides. But while this kind of writing is important, giving students the opportunity to try out new ideas, it often was not enough to improve students' writing skills.

I think every teacher wishes to have more time for what Tom Romano describes as "frequent engagement in rapid writing" where "young writers…cut loose…in high-speed chases after meaning, adventures that will take various routes, each different from the previous one" (1987, 6). Sadly, no writing assessment has yet asked for kids to show off their best "high-speed chase" writing.

Every year, the state writing assessment was our finish line. Each student had to cross that line using a specific writing prompt and rubric. Of course, I tried shortcuts to prepare students: clever acronyms, posters titled "5 Steps to a 5" or "The Writing Hamburger," even tutoring sessions. This is the reality of teaching writing. In the end, the acronym or poster might have helped students remember the structure or components, but it didn't help my students actually do the writing and revision.

## Writing and Learning

According to the National Commission on Writing, "Research is crystal clear: Schools that do well insist that their students write every day and that teachers provide regular and timely feedback" (2003, 28). Students need practice and explicit instruction for all the stages of the writing process. Further research and meta-analysis shows that in addition to devoting more time to student writing, writing instruction (specifically around the writing process), sentence construction, sentence combining, and summarization are effective classroom practices and can lead to increased comprehension of content-area texts (Graham and Perin 2007; Graham and Herbert 2010).

USING SHORT TEXTS FOR WRITING AND REVISING

Writing in any class helps students better understand the content. Focusing on producing short texts, especially in response to reading, supports students as they learn content. Graham and Herbert highlight that "having students write about a text they are reading enhances how well they comprehend it. The same result occurs when students write about a text from different content areas, such as science and social studies" (2010, 6). Adding writing to reading in such forms as summaries and analyses "has a powerful and positive impact on learning" (Shanahan 2020a, para. 21).

Students should have opportunities to write in every classroom. The short writing activities in this chapter can be used by any teacher for any content area. If you lack confidence when it comes to providing writing instruction, short writing can be a perfect solution.

## The Writing Process

In his influential book *Writing: Teachers & Children at Work*, Donald H. Graves articulated the steps of the writing process: prewriting, drafting, revision, editing, and publishing (1983). Graves describes writing as a recursive rather than linear process, meaning that writers move between the stages and return to previous stages as needed. Donald Murray, a colleague of Graves, described a similar process of prewriting, writing, and rewriting (1972).

Peter Elbow discusses the writing process more simply: "If you separate the writing process into two stages, you can exploit the opposing muscles one at a time: first be loose and accepting as you do fast early writing; then be critically tough minded as you revise what you have produced" (1998, 9).

Regardless of the names and number of the stages, the concept of the writing process or process writing remains unchanged: We think about writing. We write. We revisit what we wrote

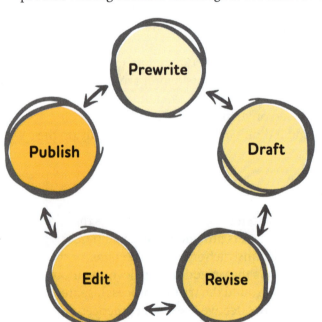

to make it better. We share what we have written. We return to the steps again and again and in any order we need.

Process writing reflects the messiness that is writing. It honors the work needed to get ideas down on paper and the energy spent untangling those words to make our ideas clear to an audience.

Research reinforces the benefits of teaching students process writing (Graham and Perin 2007; Graham et al. 2012; Sedita 2022). Students need explicit instruction in the different stages and time to practice writing in different forms and for different audiences.

Writing in the content areas improves students' understanding of the content. In addition, it improves students' reading skills and overall writing abilities (Graham and Herbert 2010). Two important reports, the *Writing Next* report (Graham and Perin 2007) and the *Writing to Read* report (Graham and Herbert 2010), recommend instruction in the writing process where students are taught "strategies for planning, revising, and editing their compositions" (Graham and Perin 2007, 4).

Little has changed in how we think about the writing process in the fifty-plus years since Graves and Murray named the stages, except for the proliferation of ways writers can publish or share their writing with the world. Graves and Murray likely did not envision a world where students can post any of their thoughts for the entire world to consume. I am eternally grateful that twelve-year-old me never had those publishing opportunities. I was no Taylor Swift. The world is better off not ever seeing the pages of my journals.

Since the writing process may not be familiar to all teachers, let's take a few moments to review its steps.

## Prewriting

Prewriting is a broad term to describe the first stage of the writing process. Prewriting can be clear and observable, like an outline or a brainstorm, or it can be less concrete, like a conversation, daydreaming, or even doodling.

The goal of prewriting is for students to find a topic and direction. Writers can return to prewriting as often as they need. When the ideas a student has in prewriting don't pan out, they need to return to prewriting to work out new ideas. When a writer realizes the three reasons that were in the outline are really just two, it is back to prewriting to decide what comes next.

Prewriting ideas include engaging prompts, novel approaches, and innovative technologies. However, prewriting is personal. What works for one writer doesn't work for all writers. Not every student is helped by a graphic organizer. Technology can be a great resource for some but a distraction for others. With all the topics in the world to write about, there is no reason every writer needs to follow the same path.

Not all prewriting has to lead somewhere. If a prompt or idea doesn't resonate, writers will run out of things to say quickly. It is okay for students to abandon a topic or idea. It is just fine to spend only a couple of minutes on a topic before moving on to the next thing. But is also important to help students move from prewriting to the next stage of the writing process. Penny Kittle writes, "As seriously as I take free writing in notebooks, I take just as seriously the need to move beyond it" (2008, 54). If a student's writer's notebook is filled with only a few sentences jotted down as part of each day's warm-up, they never get the challenge of revising and editing ideas.

## Drafting

As students move out of prewriting and into drafting, there is still lots of space for messiness. The space in between prewriting and drafting can also be a gray area. Lots of prewriting can look like drafting.

In this stage, the writer's thoughts begin to take shape. Ideas turn into sentences and sentences into paragraphs. Writers might grapple with the audience and genre, the organization and content. As Joyce Armstrong Carroll and Edward Wilson note, "In prewriting students find meaning; in writing they find form" (2019, 38). Prewriting gets the ideas out, but where those ideas go is a job for the drafting phase.

Students may benefit from writing conferences with either teachers or peers during this stage. When a student writer reads their draft aloud to a partner or teacher, it gives power to their writing. It also allows students to hear their mistakes and correct them. Student writers should feel comfortable sharing their writing and asking for feedback from others. They need to know they can ask for help when the writing isn't working. Design safe spaces for writing conversations. Help students understand that developing a final draft is a process, not something that happens instantly. If their writing is always turned in, graded, and handed back without discussion, students won't become confident writers.

Many writers, especially young writers, can be hyper-focused on spelling and correctness during the drafting phase. Donald Graves first wrote about students who want everything to be perfect in *Writing: Teachers & Children at Work* (1983). Those young writers often find it hard to revise and will sacrifice content for correctness. I should note that I am fairly sure Donald Graves was talking about five-year-old me. I was, and still am, a terrible speller. I learned early on how to use easier words that I could spell correctly versus making a spelling mistake on a harder word.

Graves advises teachers to model mistakes with our own writing, making errors in the drafting phase and using the revision and editing stages to improve writing and employ conventions. "Children who have learned to revise, to treat information, language, and conventions as temporary, know they will be able to go back and deal with conventions successfully" (Graves 1983, 87). So while we should provide ample opportunities for drafting, we also need to create space for moving into the next stages: revising and editing.

## Revising

If we only ask students to revise lengthy, major assignments, they will not practice the skill of revision frequently enough to be comfortable with it. Students need to practice revision in low-stakes situations and to learn how revision can help writers refine ideas and play with language. When the task of revision is reserved for only the finest of pieces, it can become overwhelming. However, asking for small revisions on short pieces of writing allows teachers the opportunity to clarify and narrow the focus of what we are teaching and the feedback we are giving. Lemov, Driggs, and Woolway point out that it's "important to see the revision process as something that happens with all writing, all thinking, not just drafts of the essays you turn in" (2016, 161).

The idea that only bad writers must correct their writing is pervasive and follows students well into high school and beyond. Teaching the writing process helps demystify revision so that students see how simple revision is and learn that it is something that effective writers do often.

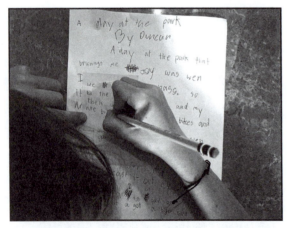

Graves describes the revision process as "reseeing," but notes that it "is not necessarily a natural act. It draws on a different source of energy, the energy of *anticipation*." (1983, 160). If we read over our writing and change a single word, we have revised. If we add an insert arrow and include a new detail, we have revised.

The goal of revision practice is to give student writers strategies they can confidently use to effect in their next writing. Revision isn't about fixing this one piece of writing; it's about building a more a confident writer. Students shouldn't be focused only on correcting the mistakes we circle. Graves reminds us about young writers: "What should never be forgotten, however, is that the *force* of revision, the *energy* for revision, is rooted in the child's voice, the urge to express" (1983, 160).

## Editing

Perhaps you remember daily language practice, when your teacher posted a sentence filled with errors and you were asked to correct the errors. All the errors. So many errors. Everything was wrong with that sentence. You shouted out revision ideas without any real knowledge of why the word *grandma* should be capitalized or whether we should be using *affect* or *effect*. Unfortunately, decades of research show that traditional, formal grammar instruction focused on correcting the errors of others has a negligible and even a negative impact on student writing (Braddock, Lloyd-Jones, and Schoer 1963; Anderson 2007; Graham and Perin 2007). As author and professor Stanley Fish writes, "You can know what the eight parts of speech are, and even be able to apply them correctly, and still not understand anything about the way a sentence works" (2012, 19).

So, then, what does editing mean during the writing process? This final step before a text meets its audience is to make the piece readable and ensure our meaning is clear. Asking students to return to their own writing to practice editing strengthens both the writing and the writer. According to Carroll, students benefit when they learn grammar by revising their own writing: "Their sentences hold intrinsic meaning and purpose for them, so students are motivated to make their writing better" (2011, 5).

Editing is not about the teacher circling errors for students to correct. If we are the ones marking errors, students "will see the teacher as the one in control of the writing process" (Graves 1983, 231). This teacher-centered editing doesn't help writers solve problems themselves (Graves 1983).

Editing is also not about creating perfect papers devoid of any errors. Age-appropriate conventions and spelling are important, as is stretching students with new conventions based on their writing. But asking students to go back and edit their writing, without any clear reference to what they are editing for, can be so overwhelming to students that they don't make any changes. As Graves notes, "Writers of all ages can only focus on so much at a time" (1983, 241).

Our instruction for editing should focus on one clear, grade-level-appropriate skill at a time. Similar to reading in layers, we can ask students to return to their writing multiple times, looking for the correct use of one convention at a time. For example, students can check end-of-sentence punctuation first, then return to look for correct use of capital letters, but do not ask them to do both at the same time. Of course, if you have not taught or reviewed the rules of capitalization, it will be difficult, if not impossible, for students to apply them.

I have spent many classroom minutes discussing the differences between revision and editing, but the truth is that one normally leads to the other. Writers rarely make a revision without having to grapple with some editing. Kelly Gallagher acknowledges this overlapping nature of the steps: "The more I write, the more I realize that the lines between revision and editing can be blurry" (2011, 222).

# USING SHORT TEXTS FOR WRITING AND REVISING

## The Recursive Writing Process

| | |
|---|---|
| **Prewriting Ponderings** | ➔ There are different kinds of prewriting. Students can prewrite to help find a topic to write about, and they can prewrite to decide what to say about a specific topic.<br>➔ Not every piece of prewriting must lead somewhere.<br>➔ Students can return to prewriting at any time in the writing process.<br>➔ Not every kind of prewriting looks the same.<br>➔ Not everyone prewrites in the same way. |
| **Drafting Details** | ➔ Getting it down is the first step. You can't revise what you haven't written.<br>➔ Model the messiness of drafting for students. They should see that good writers scratch out, draw arrows, and make mistakes along the way.<br>➔ Students may need to return to drafting (and even prewriting!) later in the writing process if something isn't working.<br>➔ Drafting an entire piece can be overwhelming. Focus on drafting a section or paragraph of text at a time. |
| **Revision Reminders** | ➔ Revision is simply adding or deleting text or combining or rearranging pieces of text.<br>➔ Revision can happen at the paragraph level, the sentence level, or even the word level.<br>➔ Writers need explicit instruction and the time and space to try out revisions.<br>➔ To internalize strategies, writers should take time to reflect on how revisions impacted their writing. |
| **Editing Epiphanies** | ➔ Students should be held accountable only for skills we have taught and reviewed. As students learn more about how language and conventions work, their skills will develop.<br>➔ Editing is separate from content review. A writer can have strong ideas and organization but struggle with grammar conventions.<br>➔ Editing should focus on one thing at a time. Asking students to fix everything is usually an overwhelming obstacle. |
| **Publishing Pointers** | ➔ Authors need to write for authentic audiences. Knowing the audience changes how we approach the writing.<br>➔ Publishing wraps up the challenging work of the writing process.<br>➔ Comparing where their writing started with where it ended helps students see their growth as writers.<br>➔ *Publishing* means sharing your work. Publication can take many forms. |

## Publishing

When I learned the writing process as a fifth grader, students in our class were given the project of publishing books to live in the school library. The books were going to be bound in hardback, and we were allowed to draw the art for the covers. Our names would be emblazoned across the fronts. The last week of school, the librarian wheeled those bound books into our fifth grade classroom, and honestly, I have been chasing the pride and accomplishment I felt ever since. Somewhere, a copy of "The Very Good Day" may still be on a bookshelf in San Antonio.

It was years later when I learned that *publishing* simply means "finishing and sharing." Writing doesn't have to be bound to be "published." Sharing with your class or your shoulder partner is a form of publishing. It is about celebrating the work and sharing the writing with the world, even if the world is an elementary school library like mine in San Antonio, Texas.

# The Role of AI in Writing Instruction

The launch of ChatGPT in late 2022 opened a new chapter on how technology can impact classrooms and instruction. Artificial intelligence, or AI, offers new and unique ways to make reading and writing simpler and more streamlined. According to *Artificial Intelligence and the Future of Teaching and Learning,* "AI could help teachers to customize and personalize materials for their students, leveraging the teacher's understanding of student needs and strengths" (U.S. Department of Education Office of Educational Technology 2023, 33).

AI can provide rich mentor texts for students to read and analyze. It can also help teachers create writing prompts for students. In addition, AI-generated writing samples offer opportunities for whole-class revision based on the writing of a "computer" classmate.

Another area of promise is using AI to provide feedback on student writing. Feedback generated from AI programs can be timely and specific; however, there are still some limitations with current (early) forms of AI. Computer scoring and human scoring notice different things when analyzing student writing (U.S. Department of Education 2023). AI-generated feedback may focus more on key words or length, whereas human scoring has a better grasp of nuance and meaning. "Due to these limitations, we must continue to emphasize a human in the loop foundation for AI-enhanced formative assessment. AI may support but not replace high-quality, human-led processes and practices of formative assessment in schools" (U.S. Department of Education 2023, 40).

As we learn more about how to utilize AI in instruction in ethical and positive ways, early guidance from the Department of Education emphasizes the importance of humans "firmly at the center" of all use of AI in teaching and learning (2023, 53). The role of the educator will continue to be to validate the information and resources AI produces and to support students with fair and ethical use of AI tools.

## LEVERAGING AI TO ENHANCE STUDENT WRITING

AI tools can serve as helpful collaborators for both teachers and students in the writing process. With capabilities ranging from brainstorming ideas to refining grammar and style, AI can empower students by functioning like a writing center, peer editor, or tutor. Tools that suggest vocabulary or prompt students with sentence starters can support prewriting, while AI-driven grammar checkers and feedback systems offer immediate, specific feedback. This allows students to focus on content and clarity, helping them see their writing improve in real time. Interacting with AI can help reluctant learners ask questions and get support they may be too shy or too scared to ask for in class.

Teachers can also integrate activities that critique AI-generated content. Together, students might analyze AI-created summaries or outlines, evaluating what's missing. Alternatively, ask AI to apply a lens to a familiar topic—like a favorite book—and have students assess its accuracy. Students can also compare AI-generated bibliographies to academic sources to gauge reliability. By integrating AI into writing tasks, educators can help students effectively employ these tools, encouraging them to approach revision and editing with enthusiasm and independence.

—Kara Ball, National Teacher of the Year finalist and author of
*50 Strategies for Teaching STEAM Skills*

# SHORT WRITING AND REVISION STRATEGIES

"If you want to be a writer, you must do two things above all others: read a lot and write a lot. There's no way around these two things that I'm aware of, no shortcut."

—Stephen King, *On Writing* (2000)

This chapter begins with three core writing strategies. Like the core reading strategies presented previously, I used these core writing strategies almost daily in my ELA classroom. They are endlessly modifiable and can be adjusted based on your students, the time you have available, your objectives, and the text or prompt at hand. Most of the short texts students write are related to short texts they read. As such, there is a significant overlap in reading and writing skills. The truth is teachers blend these skills all the time.

The core writing strategies are followed by short writing and revision strategies that can be combined and modified to meet your students' specific needs. The most effective approach is to connect reading and writing as often as possible. Pairing strategies for reading short texts with these writing and revision techniques amplifies the reading and gives students vital practice in the writing process. These strategies also allow you to use short reading texts as mentor texts and models of powerful writing techniques.

# Core Writing Strategy #1: Micro Writing

Many teachers spend a great deal of time prewriting but much less time practicing the full writing process. I typically saved the "process writing" for the couple of times a year students wrote "big" papers. These included trips to the library for research and writing multiple drafts. Now I ask: What message did I send to students about the need to revise and edit? Are these skills we want students to use only a couple times a year? Or are they skills we want students to use every time they write for an audience?

I wanted students to practice the full writing process more often, but I didn't want to assign more big essays. Kelly Gallagher and Penny Kittle point to the need for more practice with this process. "If a student only writes 'big' essays, she is not getting enough practice to improve significantly. This pathway doesn't provide enough practice for writers" (2018, para. 4).

I also wanted students to receive more targeted and timely feedback on their writing. Yet often it took so long to grade the papers that students didn't receive feedback until weeks after the assignment began. It was hard for them to see where they grew or what they had tried as a writer.

I started experimenting with Jeff Anderson's "express-lane editing," which keeps students from getting "bogged down in the totality of all that needs fixing" by instead focusing their energy on fixing one or two key skills (2005, 47). Identifying just one technique offered a way to improve writing quickly, and I found it gave students a quick writing win.

But my students needed more support to get to the point where they were ready to edit their work. They needed help coming up with ideas to write about. I also saw the need for more reflection about revisions, so that students became aware of their impact and could use those strategies again when I wasn't around handing out markers.

Building on this, I started *micro writing*, short writing tasks that take students through the full writing process in about ten minutes. Micro writing is more than the free writing journal entries that many teachers use at the start of class. With micro writing, students practice a short piece of writing, then a small revision strategy, then share and reflect on the impact of the revision with their peers. These writing bursts gave my students a win, and they formed the building blocks for a longer piece of writing. And with a focus on short writing, I was able to quickly provide meaningful feedback.

1. **Talk It Out: Short Prewriting**
   Students take two to four minutes to chat with thought partners about the topic. This should be a conversation that gives students time to think before they write. This conversation serves as verbal prewriting, allowing students to connect thought and language. You may wish to collect a few groups' responses and record them on an anchor chart to provide students with ideas and vocabulary, or you may want to create a word wall.

SHORT WRITING AND REVISION STRATEGIES

## 2. Write It Down: Short Drafting

Students take two to four minutes to draft their thoughts. I like to use small pieces of paper for this—note cards, or large sticky notes. Students are more likely to write if the space is small. We have all experienced the horrible feeling of facing a blank page; micro writing should be about nonthreatening writing opportunities. If needed, you can tape that small paper onto a larger sheet of paper to provide more space for the next step: revision and editing.

> **Teaching Tip** Though I keep track of the time, I don't display a timer for these steps. I have found it causes more anxiety than motivation.

## 3. Refine the Idea: Small Revision and Editing

Based on the micro writing students have just completed, identify one item for students to refine. I am using the word *refine* here since this step often blurs the lines between revision and editing. The refinement activity might be an editing skill, a revision technique, or something in between. I try not to overthink naming conventions since often revision requires editing and vice versa. The skill could be something you notice that students need. It could be a language or convention skill that is part of your state standards. Or it could be a skill that you know will work well with the particular writing prompt or style.

Discuss the skill with students. They should feel confident entering this stage, with all the information they need to make the refinements. For example, if you are focusing on combining sentences, then grab that anchor chart from the lesson where you previously taught it. If you are focusing on capitalization, take a few extra minutes to review the ways authors use capital letters. With a single skill for refinement, you can provide focused teaching to support it. Remember, you aren't teaching all the grammar and mechanics here, just one small thing.

Have students take two to four minutes to refine their writing. Walk about the class, answering questions and collecting good examples to share when the time ends.

You can find lesson ideas for refining the idea in the next section. See Expand a Sentence (page 84); 10% Off Revision (page 88); Roll a Revision (page 90); and Cohesion Connectors for Writing (page 92).

## 4. Reflect on It: Small Publishing

Students then take two to four minutes to share their revised micro writing. If you are short on time, you might have writers focus only on what they changed, sharing the original and the revised portion.

Students' writing can be collected and used for formative assessment. Reviewing thirty note cards with writing focused on a single skill is far faster than responding to thirty papers. Quick feedback on short writing can be easily incorporated into the next day's teaching. If you plan to assign grades, this can also be done easily.

© Shell Education

136447—Short Texts, Big Impact **61**

## SHORT WRITING AND REVISION STRATEGIES

Regardless of the method of feedback, it is important for students to pause, set the pencils down, and look at the change they made and how it impacted their writing. This publishing phase of micro writing helps students see that refining their writing, through revision, editing, or some combination of the two, makes it stronger.

### BUILDING YOUNG WRITERS' FLUENCY

A Power Write (adapted from Graves and Kittle 2005; Gallagher 2011) is a brief, timed writing exercise where students write continuously for a set period (typically three to ten minutes) about a specific topic or prompt. This strategy builds writing fluency and confidence by emphasizing quantity over quality and removing the pressure of editing during the writing process.

For young children, the Power Write adapts to their developmental level: Students can draw and write continuously for three to five minutes about familiar topics like favorite toys or recess activities. Teachers encourage invented spelling and drawing to build confidence, allowing students to switch between both modes of expression during the time limit. An even more simplified version involves list-making for five minutes. Students practice "brave spelling" to write as many words as they can within content-area topics (birds, space, etc.) or simple categories such as "foods." Students count the number of words they spelled at the end of the five minutes and try to get even more words in the next Power Write. Another adaptation uses photographs, where students label as many items as they can identify.

Throughout all versions, students are encouraged to use their phonetic knowledge, stretching out sounds and spelling bravely and quickly. Writing fluency empowers students to capture their thoughts quickly on paper, building stamina and automaticity. When ideas flow rapidly, students can dedicate more cognitive energy to expanding their writing rather than struggling with basic transcription.

—Katie Schrodt, associate professor, Middle Tennessee State University

SHORT WRITING AND REVISION STRATEGIES

# Core Writing Strategy #2: Mentor Texts, Anchor Charts, and Writer's Notebooks

Three components are vital to supporting your students as they grow as writers. These components are connected like pearls on string: mentor texts, anchor charts, and writer's notebooks. We use mentor texts to show students strong examples of writer's craft. We distill that learning onto anchor charts. Students then collect and try those techniques in their writer's notebooks.

## Mentor Texts

Examining short texts or a short portion of text for author's craft impacts both student writing and student reading. For more than a generation, we have known about the power of model, or mentor, texts. The seminal *Writing Next* report lists the study of model texts as one of the top eleven instructional strategies for impacting adolescent writing (Graham and Perin 2007).

Using mentors and models helps student writers learn how authors create meaning and see how they can make choices that have impact. Strategies like Zoom In (see page 19) focus on unpacking the moves an author made when crafting a text. Seeing a technique used effectively in a published work gives students context and concrete examples. Stanley Fish, author of *How to Write a Sentence: And How to Read One* (2012), reminds us that "practice in the analyzing and imitating of sentences is also practice in the reading of sentences" (9).

I often provided copies of small snippets of mentor text that students could glue on a page of their writer's notebooks. But student memory is fleeting. One time, a student claimed his previous year's teacher never taught him commas. I was that teacher, so I knew that wasn't the case! To make the writing skills and techniques we were unpacking concrete and a bit more permanent, I relied on anchor charts.

## Anchor Charts

Anchor charts are more than just wall decorations. They are class-created visual representations of learning. Students are "more apt to notice and utilize anchor chart information when created together in the classroom" (Gentry, McNeel, and Wallace-Nesler 2014, 31). Their proximity in the classroom means students are surrounded by reminders and teachers have examples on hand at all times.

Are we seeing an author use a technique we have already discussed? We take a look at the chart. Is a student asking a question about something we have covered? Head over to the poster. An anchor chart can serve as a collection of techniques an author might use (see "What Can We Delete?" or "Crafting Cohesion" in appendix B). Anchor charts can also remind students of conventions, such as capitalization rules or dialogue punctuation.

Be thoughtful about anchor charts so that only the most relevant ideas and examples fill the room at any given time. Here are some general principles to keep in mind:

- Create anchor charts *with* your students *while* they are learning. Sure, you could probably make nicer ones with multiple colors and a font traced from the internet,

© Shell Education

136447—Short Texts, Big Impact **63**

# SHORT WRITING AND REVISION STRATEGIES

but they won't be owned by students in the same way. Writing and learning are messy. Anchor charts can be too.

- Use examples from students' reading. It helps anchor learning when you can say, "Remember when we read ____ and the author ____?"
- Refer to anchor charts often. If you never refer to them, neither will your students.
- Add to anchor charts as new examples arise. They should not be static posters you put up in August and take down in May. They should reflect the new learning the class does all year long.

## Writer's Notebooks

Anchor charts are a useful tool, but to make writing techniques real, students need a place to try them out. I recommend using writer's notebooks. My students used composition books, but spiral notebooks or digital notebooks also work.

Writer's notebooks give students a low-pressure place to store their writing and explore writing techniques over an entire school year. Students use notebooks for brainstorming ideas, completing quick writes, trying revision techniques, capturing short texts they have read, and recording short texts they have written. There are many resources to support building and maintaining writer's notebooks, but I have found the simpler the better. When there were too many requirements, I ended up feeling like I was trying to get students to make their notebooks look a certain way. Instead, I wanted to focus my energy on engaging students in writing and ensuring they had a place to do so.

Writer's notebooks are effective when they are used consistently. If students use them almost daily, the notebooks become an invaluable resource. Here is what I learned from years of trial and error:

- I never worried about which side of the page students wrote on, what color they used, or what the pages looked like when they were done. I left those choices up to students.

- I rarely collected them to grade—they were students' place to explore writing and ideas. Any grade I attached was a quick completion grade. (Also, have you ever seen a teacher carting around twenty-five or more notebooks? Miserable. That is a mistake you make only one time.)

- I asked students to take them out and be ready to use them almost every day. Anytime I wanted students to jot down a few thoughts, I directed them to "find some space in your notebook and get started."

- If students moved to different rooms during the day, I had them store their notebooks in my classroom. Although I wanted to teach students to be responsible, the battle over getting them to bring notebooks to class every day was not worth fighting. We needed to get into the day's learning as quickly and painlessly as possible.

- Students glued or taped samples of text or notes into their notebooks, especially mentor texts. The notebooks provided a place to analyze writing and imitate writing techniques.

- Some teachers have students create a table of contents, number the pages, or incorporate a left side/right side model. The left side of the notebook is for input, where students take notes and paste texts they read; the right side is for output, where students record their writing and thinking. Note: I tried these methods, but they took more time than I wanted. I adopted a far more open "just find some space" model.

- In some instances, I prompted students to create their own anchor charts in their notebooks. Designing your own writing reminders can be a powerful form of memory consolidation.

- If you are using digital notebooks, you or your students can insert photos of anchor charts and examples of mentor texts onto the pages and use digital sticky notes or the comments function to try out revision and editing techniques.

With the goal of creating a classroom space for readers and writers, I used mentor texts, anchor charts, and writer's notebooks daily as the foundation of my instruction. These three tools are flexible and honor student voice and choice. They helped build my classroom as a place of exploration and celebration of the written word.

# Core Writing Strategy #3: Sticky Note Revision

I am convinced that my students thought that one of the steps of the writing process is *revisonandediting,* which is Latin for "just copy it over neatly on good paper." Asking students to make any real change to their writing was always a challenge.

According to students, here are a few reasons why revision is their least favorite part of writing:

- "I never started writing it in the first place."
- "I wrote it. It is perfect. I will change nothing."
- "Only kids who wrote it wrong the first time have to go back to correct it."
- "I revised it in my head as I went."
- "I don't know how to revise it."
- "I don't know grammar."
- "It takes too long."

Since revision is a painful process for many student writers, I like to use the strategy that parents everywhere have used to get their kids to try brussels sprouts and zucchini: just try one bite. I asked students to just try the revision strategy on a sticky note. A sticky note is temporary. It means the student is trying out an idea and is not required to change their writing. Students can choose to keep, move, or ignore the revision altogether once they "try just one bite."

From the teacher lens, a sticky note revision lets us quickly confirm that students tried a revision strategy. We can walk around the room to check students' progress as they write. As we peek over their shoulders looking at sticky notes, we can quickly assess and note where the student is in mastery and understanding. I used a dry-erase marker on a laminated copy of my seating chart to make notes.

This in-the-moment formative assessment gives teachers the opportunity to redirect when needed, push students for more, or simply encourage them. I carried stamps and stickers to add to sticky notes from time to time. No one ever outgrows the joy of a scratch-and-sniff sticker. You can learn more about short assessments and feedback in part 3.

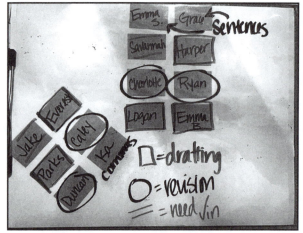

SHORT WRITING AND REVISION STRATEGIES

# The Three-Word Summary Sentence

When it comes to student achievement, summarization has a high effect size, which means it is an important classroom strategy for supporting students as both readers and writers (Dean et al. 2012; Graham and Perin 2007; National Reading Panel 2000). Yet students often struggle to write summary statements, as that requires them to "identify what material to keep and what to omit" (Dean et al. 2012, 80). The three-word summary sentence distills the requirement even further by limiting the starting summary to only three words.

Writing summary sentences after reading a short text has several benefits. It gives the entire class a common topic to write on, keeping the "I don't know what to write about" refrain to a minimum. The writing task is small and contained: even the most reluctant writer can jot three words on a sticky note. And though I often use the three-word summary sentence as a starting place for revision activities, it can also be a lightning-fast assessment of students' understanding.

Limiting the summary to a three-word sentence allows students to strip it down to its core components: a subject, a verb, and an object. Jeff Anderson (2005) presents a similar strategy, the "Two-Word Sentence Smack Down," which asks students to pick the subject and verb out of existing sentences from mentor texts. Stanley Fish (2012) discusses how three-word sentences help writers practice the logical structure and relationship between words in a sentence.

The Three-Word Summary Sentence focuses students on the most critical point of a text, while also providing an opportunity to discuss good writing at the sentence level. Joan Sedita, creator of the Writing Rope, emphasizes the need for direct, explicit instruction in sentence building and syntax (2022); this is a natural follow-up as part of a three-word summary lesson.

1. Complete a first read of the text.

2. Give each student a sticky note.

3. Ask students to write a three-word summary sentence of the text. Students may ask if they can use a contraction or if articles like *a*, *an*, and *the* count. I allow all those exceptions, and I enjoy that they are thinking critically and asking about them.

4. Share, compare, and post student sentences. Posting sentences in a chart that shows the subjects and predicates makes it easier to compare sentence components.

| Subject | Predicate (Verb + Object) |
|---|---|
| Castellanos | saved people. |
| He | helped others. |
| Mandl | was rescued. |

*Teacher Talk:* *Let's take a look at the different verbs we used for our summary sentences. Which verb is the strongest? Which verb is the most descriptive and precise? Is it stronger to say* he saved *or* he helped?

© Shell Education

SHORT WRITING AND REVISION STRATEGIES

> **Teaching Tip** Take advantage of a possible teachable moment by making sure students have complete sentences, each with a subject and predicate. A three-word sentence is one of the simplest pieces of writing that can be created. Discuss and review the components of a simple sentence as needed.

## Make It Better
Choose one of the three-word sentences to work with for the Expand a Sentence revision activity (page 84).

## Make It Happen at Any Level

| Emerging Readers and Writers (K–2) | Multilingual Learners |
|---|---|
| Complete this activity as a whole class after reading a short text. Work together to develop a few three-word summary sentences. You can scaffold this further by providing the subject of the sentence and having students finish the sentence with the verb and object. | Use this streamlined writing activity to introduce, review, or practice subject-verb agreement. |

SHORT WRITING AND REVISION STRATEGIES

# Social Media Thesis

The thesis statement is the foundation of nonfiction writing. This important sentence goes by different names depending on the age of the writer and mode of writing. It might be called the topic sentence, the central idea, a controlling idea, the main idea, the lead, the argument, or the claim. Regardless of the name, this one sentence gives unity and direction to the writing. Kenneth Bruffee calls it the "one sentence…that says exactly what the paper says" (1972, 43). Joyce Armstrong Carroll and Edward E. Wilson call it "the writer's promise to the reader" (2012, 30).

> This activity pairs nicely with an opinion/argument text such as "Homework: Helpful or Harmful?" (see page 111 for the full text).

Without a clear thesis, writing is adrift and aimless. A clear thesis statement is no accident. They take work to write and revise. All the details in the piece should connect back to it somehow. Many writers find themselves with an evolving thesis—one that starts in one place, but it ends up somewhere else. And while we can use writing to work out our thinking, informational or argumentative writing should have a unifying thesis or claim that clearly states what the author intends to accomplish.

This short writing activity gives the thesis statement full focus. Using paper sentence strips means no technology is required. Crafting a thesis like an anonymous social media post makes the revision process a little anonymous as well, since students won't know who posted which statement as they provide feedback.

1. After reading a short text, propose an argumentative prompt for students to consider. For example, "Should classrooms stop assigning homework?"

2. Start by explaining what a thesis statement is: a single sentence near the beginning of a text that explains what the entire text will be about. In argumentative writing, a thesis is the author's opinion or viewpoint. In informational writing, it is the main idea or focus.

*Teacher Talk: Many social media posts are opinions, claims, or theses. They are short pieces of writing with the writer's thought or opinion on a topic. Today, you will focus on writing and revising your own thesis statement in the form of a social media post.*

3. Give each student a sentence strip. Have them create a unique design or icon—like that of a social media profile—on the left end of the sentence strip, instead of writing their name. It should be something the authors can draw quickly. As writers "post" their statements, they can also have a bit of anonymity.

4. Have students respond to the prompt by writing their opinion in a single sentence. The response should take a stand and be as succinct and clear as possible.

   For example: *Classrooms should stop assigning homework since it has little impact on learning.*

5. Ask students to post their statements on the board. With yes/no issues like this one, you may wish to divide the board into two sides and have students place their posts in one category or the other.

© Shell Education

136447—Short Texts, Big Impact **69**

SHORT WRITING AND REVISION STRATEGIES

6. Once everyone has posted, work with your students to choose some to revise together. A variety of revisions are likely possible depending on student needs. You may focus on eliminating wordiness, playing with the syntax, or refining the point.

   The class revised the homework thesis to add the subordinate clause as a concession to the argument. *While homework can provide practice, classrooms should stop assigning homework since it has little impact on learning.*

7. Discuss how the revisions make the post stronger. In the example above, the class restructured the sentence and took a clearer stand.

**Student social media summaries posted on the class wall for revision.**

## Make It Better
Sentence strips can be pricey, but they are perfect for this activity. I had each student put their unique "profile" image on the left end of the strip and their name on the back. Then I laminated the sentence strips and reused them repeatedly with dry erase markers. When we finished an activity with the strips, I simply clipped them together with a binder clip and hung them up for another day!

## Make It Happen with Any Text
Students can do this work with any genre of mentor text, or even no text at all. Opinion/argument is my favorite place to start, since even young students often have strong opinions.

Students can also compare how various news sources write headlines on the same topic. This reading activity highlights how writers can shape a message with small changes to word choice and syntax.

## Make It Happen at Any Level

| Emerging Readers and Writers (K–2) | Experienced Readers and Writers (6–12) |
|---|---|
| While young writers may not be ready for social media, they have seen it in the world around them. Provide a visual option using an Instagram-type image or a meme to ask an opinion question, and then work together to write a response. | My older students *loved* reading the social media posts of famous people and revising them to make them better. Students brought in screenshots of poorly worded or confusing posts, and we worked to revise them. This revision was a lot more fun than any daily oral language sentence! |

SHORT WRITING AND REVISION STRATEGIES

# The Six-Word Memoir

There are writing contests, websites, and books devoted to quippy, poetic six-word memoirs. Famous and not-so-famous people contribute their entries. In *Not Quite What I Was Planning* (2006), the editors at *Smith Magazine* first published winners from its "battle of brevity" writing contest. You can see compelling examples and the ongoing contests at sixwordmemoirs.com.

Using six-word memoirs as mentor texts provides opportunities for rich conversations about a writer's clever word choice or use of punctuation. Changing just one word to be more precise or biting can breathe life and mystery into the memoir. Many six-word memoirs tell only part of the story and hold just a bit of tension in the words.

The six-word memoir assignment is a class favorite. This short writing challenge is a great start-of-the-year activity to get to know students. I had my students write their memoirs on sentence strips that we displayed in the room just in time for open house. You can also use the idea of telling a story in six words for other purposes.

1. Start by exploring mentor texts of other six-word memoirs and talking about what makes them work. You might create an anchor chart or list of techniques that writers are using to make a six-word memoir work. For example, did they use a contraction? A precise word? A dash or a colon? Other punctuation?

2. Invite students to write their own stories in just six words. Though the original idea is for a memoir, you might ask students to write six words that focus on a part of the school year, a hobby, or something they are good at. Or you can keep the prompt open and let students select any topics they want.

3. Some students may jump right in with writing, and other students may need some additional support to get started. Have those students start by brainstorming words that describe them or things they enjoy.

4. Have students take the words and ideas they brainstormed and turn them into one sentence with no word limit.

5. Encourage students to revise, sculpt, and refine their sentences into six words using some of the techniques the class discovered in six-word mentors.

© Shell Education

136447—Short Texts, Big Impact  **71**

SHORT WRITING AND REVISION STRATEGIES

6. Share, post, and applaud the writing. Point out some of the techniques students used to craft the response.

### Favorite Six-Word Memoirs from Friends

- Birthday tacos: better than birthday cake.
- Popcorn's the best part of movies.
- When exploring with Grandpa, time flies.
- Want adventure? Splash in the mud.
- Always moving, can we stay put?
- Turn around, we forgot the milk.
- Where's the bookstore? I need books!
- Riding bikes until my legs hurt.
- A theatre kid afraid to talk.
- Ironically, writing teacher with writer's block.

## Make It Better

Entire genres are devoted to telling stories with short writing. Search for *micro-fiction*, *flash fiction*, and the *55-word story* at bookstores and online for amazing examples and mentor texts. Both flashfictionmagazine.com and sixwordmemoirs.com showcase crowdsourced writing and offer contests each year.

## Make It Happen with Any Text

Short writing can also be used for content-related assignments. You might ask students to summarize an event or process in six words. Or have them write a six-word response to a short text passage. Students can also write a six-word memoir for a character in a literary text.

SHORT WRITING AND REVISION STRATEGIES

# Song (Re)writer

"All you have to do is grab it. Then shape it like clay. Prune it like a garden. And then wish on every lucky star or pray to whatever power you believe in that it might find its way out into the world and make someone feel seen, feel understood, feel joined in their grief or heartbreak or joy for just a moment."
—Taylor Swift on songwriting, 2022 Nashville Songwriter Awards

Lyrics stay with us more readily than essays or nonfiction texts. Who hasn't belted out "Shake It Off" while at a stoplight? (Taylor's version only, of course.) Or joined in for a "Livin' on a Prayer" sing-along? I may not remember what I ate for dinner last night, but I can tell you every single word of R.E.M.'s "It's the End of the World as We Know It (And I Feel Fine)."

We all have songs that speak to us, our own personal "walk-up songs." For some of us, the lyrics are almost a sacred text. And it is this passion that makes song lyrics the perfect small text to revise. When students connect deeply with the original words, any change to those words is often deeply felt as well. Through the revision, students can compare well-loved lyrics with a revised version, and in doing so, see the impact of word choice.

This activity supports both reading and writing and is a unique way to show the benefits and limits of using a thesaurus for revision. Song (Re)writer asks students to play with words to see the powerful impact diction can have on writing. As Jeff Anderson says, "Students need to know it is ok to start small…. They come to know their own power to select the best words, creating both clarity and beauty while making meaning" (2011, 221).

1. Tell students to bring the lyrics to a favorite song to class. (Or select a song to work on with the whole class.) If students are bringing lyrics, caution them to select songs with school-appropriate lyrics.

2. Have students revise the lyrics using synonyms for some of the words. They don't have to replace all of the words, and the words don't have to rhyme, but encourage students to try to stay close to the structure of the original text. Model with a few lines of your own chosen song or with a few lines from a well-known song.

### Example Song (Re)writer

| Original Song Lyric<br>from Francis Scott Key's<br>"The Star-Spangled Banner," 1814 | Revised Song Lyric |
|---|---|
| *O say can you see by the dawn's early light*<br>*What so proudly we hailed at the twilight's last gleaming,*<br>*Whose broad stripes and bright stars through the perilous fight*<br>*O'er the ramparts we watched, were so gallantly streaming?* | Did you see this morning?<br>We were so proud and happy to see that when the sun came up,<br><br>Our flag had made it through the dangerous battle,<br><br>and we could see it waving bravely over the fort. |

© Shell Education

## SHORT WRITING AND REVISION STRATEGIES

3. Ask students to reflect on their new lyrics. How did the song change? Why does it feel different even if it means the same thing?

> **Teaching Tip** This difference in feeling is often a difference in **tone.** Authors can change the tone of their writing by changing the words they use. This purposeful word choice is called *diction*.

4. Explain that good writers choose their words purposefully. Songwriters have many words to choose from, but only specific words make it into the final song. How do we choose the right word? How does a song change when we change the lyrics?

5. Explain that when we write, we must consider our own words carefully. There is more than one way to express our ideas, but the overall feeling or tone changes when we change the words.

"Here's to hoping you're worth
all my time"
            -Let It Happen, Gracie Abrams

hoping - anticipating - aspiring

Worth - caliber - evaluation - merit

time - stint - duration - epoch

Here's to aspiring ^that you
merit all of my epoch.

SHORT WRITING AND REVISION STRATEGIES

## Make It Better

If you choose a historic song like "The Star-Spangled Banner," you have an amazing opportunity to teach students about its historical context.

## Make It Happen at Any Level

| Experienced Readers and Writers (6–12) |
| --- |
| Older students like to bring in their own songs. Before having students revise, ask them to do a quick write about how their song speaks to them. Then, instead of revising their own lyrics, have students trade lyrics with partners for revision. When they get their revised songs back, ask them to write about how the changes to the song impact their feelings about it. |

© Shell Education

136447—Short Texts, Big Impact  **75**

SHORT WRITING AND REVISION STRATEGIES

# Infographics

Infographics are a hybrid genre: a combination of visual elements and words to convey information. As with traditional informational texts, authors of infographics consider the audience and main idea. Then, through the effective use of images, graphics, colors, and shapes, infographics blend short texts and visual elements. By incorporating elements of design, authors of infographics can use fewer words to convey their message.

It is challenging to read dense text filled with facts, dates, and numbers. Not only is it difficult to comprehend, it is also hard to identify the most relevant pieces of information. Most of the information transmitted to the brain is visual, in part because visuals are processed faster than text (Weissman 2022).

Infographics are not new. The history of the infographic goes back more than 100 years. According to Clive Thompson, "Scientists and thinkers found themselves drowning in their own flood of data—and to help understand it, they invented the very idea of infographics" (2016, para. 4). Thompson charts the evolution of these tools for mentally visualizing data and explains, "We live in an age of Big Data. If we're going to understand our complex world, one powerful way is to graph it" (2016, para. 3).

Infographics are used in every field and are published in newspapers, in magazines, on social media, and in advertisements. Research shows that social media postings that include infographics increase engagement and reach more than text-only postings (Oska, Lerma, and Topf 2020).

Infographics are simply another kind of informational text. The authors of infographics make choices using color, images, layout, fonts, text, and order to convey meaning quickly and memorably. These are no different than the choices authors make when crafting informational texts. VandeHei, Allen, and Roy remind creators that "clean, intuitive visuals help amplify or bring to life an important point" (2022, 141).

In this activity, students will look at published infographics as mentor texts to analyze the choices the authors made, then use what they learn to create their own infographics.

1. Share one or more texts with infographics with students. Ask the following questions to analyze the graphics:

   - What is the main idea of this infographic?
   - What facts or details are included?
   - Who is the audience? Who is the author?
   - How is the infographic designed? (e.g., Is it set up as a time line? Does it show cause and effect? Does it provide a step-by-step guide? Does it describe parts of a whole?)
   - What are the features of the infographic? (titles, sections, colors, shape, and so on)

2. Ask students, "Why do authors use infographics? What techniques do authors use when creating infographics?"

3. Complete a first read of a detail-heavy informational or procedural text with few or no infographics.

76    136447—Short Texts, Big Impact

© Shell Education

SHORT WRITING AND REVISION STRATEGIES

> **Teaching Tip** Another option is to select a text that uses an infographic, but don't include it when you share the text with students. Later, students can compare their versions with the author's version.

4. Ask students to reenter the text to determine the main idea.

5. Have students find a section of text that feels especially dense or detailed. Zooming in on that section of text, determine how the information is organized. (Is it chronological? Parts of a whole? Procedural? Cause and effect?)

6. Tell students to each sketch a shape that can help convey the information from the text. Encourage them to consider color in their designs.

7. Ask students to distill the information into a shorter piece of text and add it to the graphic. Help students think about this by asking what details need to be included and what can be condensed.

8. Have students compare their infographics. How are they the same? How are they unique? What is effective?

## Make It Better
Make sure students understand the importance of citing sources when using research or data. This applies to infographics just as it does to other written assignments.

## Make It Happen with Any Text
Texts that are chronological, cause and effect, parts of a whole, and procedural make great infographics. Students can use infographics to summarize complex information or convey information that they are producing. Consider replacing a traditional written assignment, such as a report about an animal or a country, with an infographic.

## Make It Happen at Any Level

| Emerging Readers and Writers (K–2) | Experienced Readers and Writers (6–12) |
|---|---|
| Create infographics as a shared research and writing activity. Have students decide what animal they would like to study. Ask students what types of things they can learn about the animal (e.g., what it eats, its habitat, its characteristics, and so on). After finding the answers, students can work to create a class infographic by adding animal facts to a drawing of the animal. | Have students use online platforms to create their own infographics. Platforms such as Canva and Google Slides can make this work easy and are adding new features all the time. |

© Shell Education

136447—Short Texts, Big Impact **77**

SHORT WRITING AND REVISION STRATEGIES

# Storyboarding for Prewriting

"But Miss Carlton, I don't have anything to write about."
—Every student I ever taught

A storyboard is a visual outline. Storyboards are used for planning projects that use video, such as films, TV shows, and video games. Commercials and live productions are often sketched out like a comic strip, including dialogue, visuals, and even musical cues.

Young and emerging writers use drawings to tell their stories and convey meaning before they master the use of written words to tell their stories. For them, drawing *is* writing. As students develop writing proficiency, they replace their drawings with written words. But just because students *can* write out their stories doesn't mean we should abandon drawing in the classroom.

I first explored storyboarding after reading Joyce Armstrong Carroll's article "Drawing into Meaning: A Powerful Writing Tool." Carroll, a renowned writing educator, writes that "students should be encouraged to draw into meaning, whether as prewriting…or as initial responses to literature" (1991, 35). She adds that drawing and sketching emerge as a powerful writing tool for students of all ages.

Storyboarding is especially helpful for multilingual students. As a prewriting activity, storyboarding can "provide learners an opportunity to improve organizational and transitional skills by plotting out the main ideas of their writing through image sequencing" (Toister 2020, 127). Drawing before writing also lowers the affective filter, placing the focus and energy on coming up with the ideas instead of fighting to find the right words to express thoughts.

Taking away the pressure of finding the words can free some students to express more than they planned. Often their sketches include impressive details that might have been skipped in a first draft of writing. This activity focuses on using storyboarding for prewriting and revision to both add and organize details. You may need to reassure students that their drawings don't have to be perfect. Drawing for storyboards is not the same as drawing done as an art form (Carroll 1991).

# SHORT WRITING AND REVISION STRATEGIES

1. Show a sample storyboard with sketches of a nursery rhyme or familiar story. Carroll (2007) suggests *Little Miss Muffet* as an example of a sequential story. You can also use samples from graphic novels or comic strips.

2. Give students a storyboard template. Offer a preprinted version or have students use three to six sticky notes placed on blank paper. (See page 124 for a template.) You may wish to provide colored pencils or markers.

3. Provide a narrative writing prompt and ask students to create a storyboard response. For example: *Write about a time you faced a challenge*.

> **Teaching Tip** If you decide to have students add text under the images, have them do that after they sketch out the basic story. This will help them focus on their ideas and the story order, and they won't have to keep switching between drawing and writing.

4. After students have sketched their stories, have them pair up and share their storyboards with one another. This informal peer conference gives students the opportunity to practice telling the stories that go along with the images.

5. After each partner shares, the other student should point to the panel of the storyboard that is the best/most interesting part of the story.

6. Ask the authors to go back to that panel and add another frame that expands on the best part of the draft. At this stage I like to use the words "revise" and "draft" to emphasize that this work is part of the writing process.

7. Students continue revising their storyboards until they are ready to write. Students often ask to add, delete, rearrange, or combine panels based on their partner shares. Make extra sticky notes available for this.

8. Ask students to share any changes they made to their storyboards. In my experience, almost every student will make some sort of change to their initial storyboard, such as adding a bit of detail or some dialogue or reordering the panels. All those changes are forms of revision. Highlight the idea that writers change their ideas based on the feedback of others.

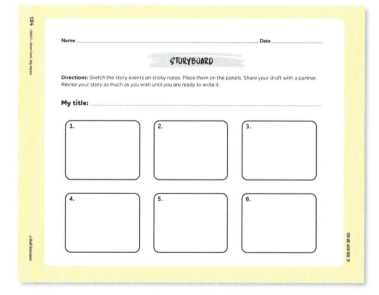

SHORT WRITING AND REVISION STRATEGIES

## Make It Better
You can also use storyboarding as a reading strategy by asking students to sketch out what they have just read as a form of summary. They can add textual support or quotations under the images to help explain the panels.

## Make It Happen with Any Text
Though storyboarding lends itself to narrative, character-driven writing adventures, it can be used anytime students start writing. Sketching informational writing looks a little different, since it often isn't sequential, but the same tenets hold true: Take away the pressure of finding the words, and let students sketch or draw their main ideas.

## Make It Happen at Any Level

| Emerging Readers and Writers (K–2) | Experienced Readers and Writers (6–12) |
|---|---|
| Use a three-panel story to start (one panel each for the beginning, the middle, and the end). Not only does this give students practice with plot structure, it also ensures there is an ending in place! (First grade students love to tell a story with no ending!)<br><br>When ready, students can add more panels to the middle as needed to tell their story, but it is helpful if they have an ending in mind before they begin adding panels. | For this age group, I prefer using sticky notes and allowing students to play around with the order by moving the panels. These students can also experiment with more sophisticated story structures, like flashbacks, or *in medias res* (starting in the middle of the story). |

SHORT WRITING AND REVISION STRATEGIES

# The Unstuck List

To paraphrase the 1972 Stealers Wheel song, getting stuck in the middle with no idea of what to do can be frustrating. To help propel my students beyond the middle, I display an anchor chart with a list of my favorite ideas for getting "unstuck." This anchor chart is a grab bag of sentence starters to help students keep the pen moving and get to the next sentence. The Unstuck List supports writers at multiple parts of the writing process, from drafting to revision.

I introduce the anchor chart early in the school year when we are doing some low-stakes writing. I have students keep a page in their writer's notebooks with the list and add to it throughout the year. This provides a consistent place students can turn to when they are stuck and need help getting going again.

> A subordinating conjunction links an independent clause (a complete sentence) and a dependent clause (an incomplete sentence). The most common subordinating conjunctions are: *as, although, after, while, when, unless, because, before, if,* and *since* (AAAWWUBBIS)

One of the easiest ways to get unstuck is to use a subordinating conjunction. Jeff Anderson recommends that students practice writing sentences that start with a subordinating conjunction (2005). If you just got a little sweaty thinking this turned into a grammar test, don't worry. You can use the subordinating conjunction without knowing what it is called.

These words are affectionately referred to by the acronym AAAWWUBBIS. Starting a sentence with a subordinating conjunction moves a writer from a simple sentence to a complex sentence. In addition to creating better syntax and greater sentence variety, using a subordinating conjunction pushes the writer to add more of their thinking to the sentence. For writing clarity, we use a comma to separate the dependent clause.

The Unstuck List gives students a way to tackle two kinds of revision: adding and rearranging details. There are other ways to start a new sentence and get out of being stuck. The box on this page shows some of my favorites, but I am always on the lookout for new ones in the writing of others.

1. Create an Unstuck List anchor chart. (See page 117 for my version of the chart.)

2. Have students produce a quick write on a topic connected to a recent reading.

   For example, if students are responding to the text "Homework: Helpful or Harmful?" (page 111), they may get stuck coming up with reasons to prove why homework is not beneficial.

3. After a few minutes of writing, ask, "How many of you have run out of things to write?"

4. Introduce the Unstuck List as a resource students can use to keep the pen moving when they are not sure they have much more to say.

> **MY FAVORITE "UNSTUCKERS"**
>
> - In the end...
> - It started with...
> - If _____, then _____
> - Just like...
> - Despite...
> - Even though...
> - Depending on...
> - In addition to...
> - And remember AAAWWUBBIS (subordinating conjunctions)!

© Shell Education

136447—Short Texts, Big Impact **81**

SHORT WRITING AND REVISION STRATEGIES

5. Invite students to return to their writing and add one more thing using an idea from the Unstuck List. The addition can be anywhere in the writing—the beginning, the middle of a sentence, or tacked on to the end. I like to have students do this work on a sticky note so it is easier to move around.

    Student Example: **Even though** homework can give students extra practice with math problems, it can also frustrate students who can't solve the math problems correctly in the first place.

6. Ask volunteers to share their additions. After each student shares, ask, "Do you like it? Will you keep it in your writing?"

> **Teaching Tip** This conversation helps reinforce that every student has personal autonomy when it comes to choices about their writing. They are the authors, after all! It is okay for students to try something and decide it doesn't fit. Using a sticky note emphasizes the idea that writers can opt to remove something they have tried.

7. Continue to refer to and use the Unstuck List anchor chart when you model your own writing. For example, I shared that I got stuck after writing this sentence: *Coffee is an important part of the day.* Using the Unstuck List, I modeled my thinking and wrote my next sentence: ***In addition to** the caffeine boost, a daily cup of coffee has other real health benefits.* Encourage students to go to the Unstuck List when they think they are done and try one thing.

## Make It Better

If you teach language arts, several mini-lessons can be based on the list, for example, comma rules, sentence structure, and parts of speech. Watch for teachable moments when you discover new ideas for the anchor chart.

## Make It Happen at Any Time

This list should be dynamic. Add ideas to it when you see them from other writers, including the students in your class. I like to display a list of choices for one semester and then swap them out with new ideas. If you use the list—adding to it, pointing out when others use it, referring to it when you write—your students will use it too.

# Make It Happen at Any Level

| Multilingual Writers | Experienced Readers and Writers (6–12) |
|---|---|
| Use a simplified list comprised mainly of coordinating conjunctions: *for, and, not, but, or, yet,* and *so,* known as FANBOYS. These can take simple sentences and elevate them into compound sentences. | Unstuckers are an effective way to keep writing, but they often can slow down or clog up the final draft. Pair this with the 10% Off Revision strategy (page 88) to show that these sentence starters might be removed from writing later during the revision process. |

SHORT WRITING AND REVISION STRATEGIES

# Expand a Sentence

Quite simply, revision is adding, deleting, rearranging, and combining details. Instead of starting at the paragraph level, I like to teach students about revising by using a three-word summary sentence (page 67). A sentence is the shortest amount of writing we can use to practice revision. I often start with a three-word summary sentence based on something we are reading. The entire class works from the same starting place, and the shared text we read to create the original sentence provides the details students need to expand it.

> The examples shown here use the text "What's Right at All Costs" (see page 108 for the full text).

In *The Writing Rope* (2022), Joan Sedita identifies activities such as sentence elaboration to instruct and practice one of the key writing skills: syntax. By adding details to an existing sentence, students see that they can improve their writing.

1. Start with a three-word summary sentence from a text students have read. This example uses the text "What's Right at All Costs" and the three-word summary sentence *He saved people*.

2. Working either with your full class or pairs, have students add details to expand the sentence. Ask, "What can we add to improve this sentence?"

   *Teacher Talk: We started with the sentence "He saved people." What is something we can add to that sentence to make it better? (Students I taught replied that we should add his name, how many people he saved, what the people were saved from, and how he saved them.)*

3. With each suggestion, ask if the detail is important to include. For example, one detail my class opted not to include was the phrase *during World War II*. As a class, we decided there was enough detail in the sentence and that the detail was not needed and felt redundant.

4. Determine where each addition should go in the sentence. For example: "Does it work better as an opening phrase? Or should we add a conjunction and make it a compound sentence?"

5. After expanding the sentence, have students reflect on why adding details can improve writing.

   *Teacher Talk: We revised our three-word sentence to create this expanded one:*
   By forging documents, Castellanos saved 40,000 Jewish people from the Nazis.
   *Which do you think is stronger? The original or the revised version? I think we have discovered that our writing can start as a simple, three-word sentence, but we can revise it and add details to make it better.*

**84** 136447—Short Texts, Big Impact

© Shell Education

## Make It Better

Be sure to use the word *revise* as you work to expand the sentence. Many students are confused about what revision really is, and this is a perfect example of just how painless it can be.

## Make It Happen with Any Text

Once students have practiced expanding a sentence from a three-word summary, they can repeat the process using their own writing in any genre. Have them highlight a short simple sentence in a draft and work to expand it in cycles by adding details.

## Make It Happen at Any Level

| Multilingual Learners |
|---|
| Multilingual students may need support as they learn where and in what order to add adjectives. The placement of adjectives in English may differ from their placement in students' home languages. |

SHORT WRITING AND REVISION STRATEGIES

# SCAMPER: One-Word Revision

For many students, revision is the most difficult part of the writing process. That single sentence took me three drafts to write, and I still don't love it. (More on that in just a bit!) To put it another way, revision is a problem to solve: How do I make this writing better?

Jeff Anderson and Deborah Dean address the fear of revision by asserting that "students need options for how to say what they want to say. They need options for revising at the sentence level" (2014, 4). Revision is often overwhelming to students who have already expended a great deal of initial energy just getting the draft down on paper. Often, students are reluctant to make changes to their writing, or quite simply, they run out of time before the final product is due. Many students avoid revision entirely because they do not know where to start.

## SCAMPER

**Substitute**—Change one word for another.

**Combine**—Combine two words into one.

**Adapt**—Borrow a word from a friend, the text, or the room.

**Magnify**—Make a word bigger, better, or more exaggerated.

**Put to Another Use**—Change the part of speech and use a word in a new way.

**Eliminate**—Delete a word.

**Rearrange**—Change the order of the words or details.

SCAMPER is an acronym for brainstorming and creative thinking (Eberle 1971). Originally designed as a series of questions to ask during brainstorming to elicit creative solutions, SCAMPER also provides a useful starting place for easing revision fear. Asking students to change just a single word of text can be an easy entry point into revision. SCAMPER offers an adjustable pathway for revision with concrete ideas for how to change just one word. Anyone can change one word!

1. After they've completed a short piece of writing, introduce students to all or part of the acronym SCAMPER. Explain that they will revisit their writing to change just one word.

2. Model the SCAMPER revision with a sample sentence. Ask students to help you make one or more of the changes to improve the sentence.

> **Example Starting Sentence:** *Revision is the most difficult part of the writing process.*
>
> **SCAMPER Revision 1:** Revision is the most **challenging** part of the writing process. (Substitute *challenging* for *difficult*.)
>
> **SCAMPER Revision 2:** The most challenging part of the writing process is **revision**. (Rearrange sentence order.)
>
> **SCAMPER Revision 3:** Revision is the most difficult part of writing. (Eliminate *process*.)
>
> **SCAMPER Revision 4:** Revision is the **hardest** part of the writing process. (Combine *most challenging* into *hardest*.)

SHORT WRITING AND REVISION STRATEGIES

3. Reflect on the impact of a change on the model sentence. Does it still hold the same meaning? Is the revised version better?

> *Teacher Talk:* *I like the change I made in revision 4 by combining two words into one. It makes what I am trying to say more direct and forceful. And while I like the idea of changing the word order in revision 2, I think I want to keep my focus on the word* revision, *so I will leave it as the first word in the sentence.*

4. Ask students to return to their own writing.
5. Invite students to use SCAMPER ideas to change just one word of their writing.
6. Share and reflect on the revisions. Ask, "Did this change make the writing better? How?"
7. Celebrate all revision attempts, including ones where a student tried to make a change but preferred their original version.

## Make It Better

Students can repeat the process as many times as they want. Not all parts of SCAMPER will work for all writers or all sentences. Remember, the goal is small: Change just one word. The bigger goal is to show students that revision is as simple as changing just one word and it improves their writing.

## Make It Happen with Any Text

I recommend displaying a SCAMPER anchor chart year-round in your classroom. You could also create small versions for students to glue into their writer's notebooks. Any time a student is stuck or only has a few minutes to revise, ask them to SCAMPER and change just one word.

## Make It Happen at Any Level

### Emerging Readers and Writers (K–2) and Multilingual Learners

Use a simplified version of SCAMPER with younger students. Emerging writers will be able to *Substitute* and *Eliminate*.

Further simplify this strategy by asking students to simply add or delete a single word. As students show proficiency with this, add strategies to a class anchor chart. Do not feel like students have to SCAMPER right away!

© Shell Education

136447—Short Texts, Big Impact **87**

SHORT WRITING AND REVISION STRATEGIES

# 10% Off Revision

Revision, at its core, is adding, deleting, combining, and rearranging ideas in writing. Though we often ask students to go back into their drafts to add more detail, we typically do not provide as much support for helping writers see what to take out.

Deleting is a simple way to improve writing. Jeff Anderson and Deborah Dean call it "one of the most useful revision decisions a writer makes," since they are "getting rid of words that aren't really doing any work" (2014, 19–20). William Zinsser's classic work *On Writing Well* urges writers to "look for clutter in your writing and prune it ruthlessly" (2001, 17). By focusing on deleting words, we can help students determine what is most important. 10% Off Revision is a strategy that gives students practice finding and deleting unnecessary words to make their writing more powerful and succinct.

1. After students complete a short bit of writing, have them each count the number of words in their draft and write it at the top of the paper.

2. Explain that revision is not only adding text, but it can also be choosing text that should be deleted. This could be words, phrases, or even whole paragraphs. Model with sample writing and ask students for help deleting words.

3. Ask students to review their own writing and try to eliminate 10 percent of the words. Have students put a bracket around words that are not necessary and could be deleted. Bracketing is an important first step that allows students to weigh whether the words are necessary before eliminating them (Zinsser 2001).

> **Teaching Tip** Giving students a percentage of text to delete (rather than a word count) makes this task naturally differentiated. Writers who are more verbose will have more words that could be deleted. You can always increase the percentage, but 10 percent is a good place to start.

4. Have students work with partners as they grapple with their deletion choices.

5. After students have completed this task, have them reflect on the changes. Ask, "Is the revised writing better? How so? What strategies did you use to make the writing more concise?"

## Make It Better

Like with all revision strategies, students need time to reflect after trying 10% Off. As students share their experiences, create an anchor chart of strategies for deleting and/or create a list of items to consider for deletion. Building an anchor chart from students' learning creates a guide they can return to in the future.

SHORT WRITING AND REVISION STRATEGIES

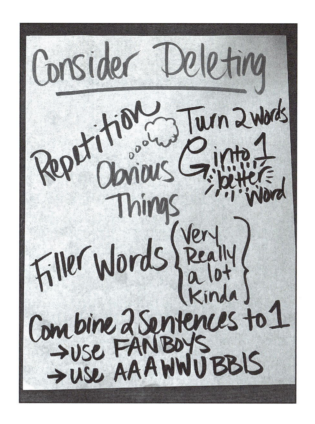

## Make It Happen at Any Level

| Emerging Readers and Writers (K–2) | Experienced Readers and Writers (6–12) |
|---|---|
| Young writers have some favorite words they like to use—specifically *I* to start a sentence and *and* to add more and more details.<br><br>Consider asking students to circle the times they use these favorite words and practice revising some of them to make them better.<br><br>For example: *I went to the park, and I ate ice cream and I played on the swings and I went on the slide.*<br><br>Students could circle all the *ands* used in the example to see if they can try to say the same thing another way. | I have used a similar strategy to remove passive voice or "to be" verbs. Many sentences containing *a, is, was, were, be, being,* and *been* can be improved through revision.<br><br>Example: *Many sentences can be improved through revision.*<br><br>Revision: *Improve writing with revision.*<br><br>I ask students to total the "to be" verbs in their pieces and reduce the total by 50 percent. It can be a challenge, but it often pushes students toward better word choice and syntax. |

SHORT WRITING AND REVISION STRATEGIES

# Roll a Revision

Peter Elbow calls revising "the hardest task of all" (1998, 121). He writes about the fruitlessness of "revising as you write and thus judging and correcting and trying to throw away every sentence while you are in the act of trying to write it" (121). Often, to avoid the revision stage, students will tell me, "Oh, I revised it in my head as I wrote it."

Roll a Revision is a way for students to try different revision techniques and engage in small-group collaboration and conversation. After students revise, they have an opportunity for sharing and immediate feedback. At the very least, it offers students a chance to hear their own words aloud. At its best, Roll a Revision puts the focus back on what revision is about: making meaning clearer for the reader. A small-group audience to listen to each change and provide feedback makes the process less scary and lonely.

Just like its companion strategy, Roll a Response (page 41), Roll a Revision is designed to be an easy way to get students engaged in revision. It is quick, low-stakes, and student-centered. This activity can be done quickly to practice and apply any recent mini-lessons.

1. Place students in small groups of four or five. Each student will be working with a piece of their own recent writing. Each group needs a number cube, sticky notes, and one *Roll a Revision* activity sheet (page 122).

2. Have students take turns rolling the cube to see what revision each of them will try out.

3. Each student selects a portion of their writing to try out the revision and writes their revision on a sticky note.

4. Students share and reflect on the revisions with their small group by reading the original and revised versions. The group members discuss which version they like better and why.

5. Repeat and modify the process as time allows.

## Make It Better

There are endless modifications to this strategy. To keep things interesting in your classroom, try one of these options:

- Provide twelve revision ideas and use two number cubes.

- Allow students to add items to the revision list.

- Allow groups to compete for "best impact" or "most changed" at each round.

- From my former students: Provide small whiteboards for students to offer Olympics-style scoring for each revision.

- Have each student try the revision on *another* student's paper.

90    136447—Short Texts, Big Impact

© Shell Education

## Make It Happen with Any Text

You can modify the revision options to match the genre and skills with which you are working. One thing I liked to do was look at the writing and reading standards and create an option that corresponded with each key standard. For instance, for a standard about using figurative language in writing, one of the revision strategies could be to add a simile or metaphor.

## Make It Happen at Any Level

Consider your options by taking a close look at the state writing standards for revision at your grade level. For example, first and second grade writers might roll a revision to add a fact to their informational text. Students in fourth or fifth grade might be asked to revise a transition word to show the connection between ideas.

SHORT WRITING AND REVISION STRATEGIES

# Cohesion Connectors for Writing

Cohesion both between sentences and between paragraphs creates unity, which William Zinsser calls "the anchor of good writing" (2001, 50). For developing writers, however, creating cohesive writing roughly translates to sticking *firstly*, *secondly*, or *lastly* at the start of each paragraph.

Student writers need to learn to build cohesion line by line. Asking students to notice the ways authors connect ideas in mentor texts gives students a roadmap for connecting ideas in their own writing. Thus, this strategy often follows the work done in Layered Annotations: Cohesion Connectors (page 29). After identifying cohesion connectors in a mentor text, students are ready to examine their own work for these connectors.

Since cohesion can be a somewhat nebulous concept, it helps to create a visual representation for this complex skill. Using a visual model for revision and editing is part of a set of strategies Joyce Armstrong Carroll calls "ratiocination," which is when "students reexamine their own writing" using codes and color (2011, 6). The brain "both perceives and creates patterns," so by drawing the links and connections in a mentor text, students can see the pattern of what cohesive writing looks like visually (2011, 19). Making cohesion connectors in their own writing gives students a visual pattern they can examine. Do they have threads connecting one sentence to the next? Do they see connections from one paragraph to the next?

For this strategy, students will use writing they have produced and find their own cohesion connectors from sentence to sentence and idea to idea. The writing piece for this task should be more than simply ideas jotted down. It should have three or more paragraphs so students can work on connecting ideas.

1. Explain to students that good writers make sure that their readers have what Jeff Anderson (2011) calls a "smooth and steady path" to follow. Good writing is linked sentence to sentence so the reader does not get confused.

2. Explore or review ways writers create a flow of ideas (or information) from sentence to sentence and paragraph to paragraph. (See page 114 for a sample anchor chart for Crafting Cohesion.)

3. Have students review their writing, starting with the first sentence and finding how it connects to the second sentence. Ask them to circle the item in the first sentence and the item in the second sentence that are connected, then draw a line to connect them.

   In the following example, student author Emma Brown is telling a story about a lost puppy. We meet the dog first through a "Bark! Bark!" that we hear at the door. Emma uses gray to connect "dog," "poor dog," "your owner," and "pup" together. Emma also uses yellow to connect Ruby (her main character) and Ruby's family.

92   136447—Short Texts, Big Impact   © Shell Education

# SHORT WRITING AND REVISION STRATEGIES

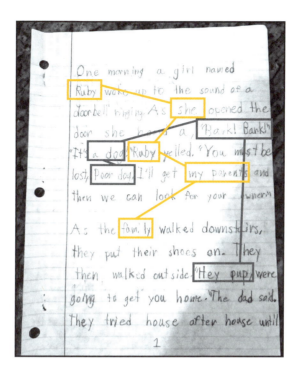

4. Students continue connecting sentences and paragraphs with cohesion connectors.
5. Ask students to reflect: *Is there something that connects each sentence to the next? Each paragraph to the next? Is it strong enough to be clear for a reader? Should I revise?* Students can refer to the anchor chart created when they analyzed the ways authors create cohesion to help revise their own writing.

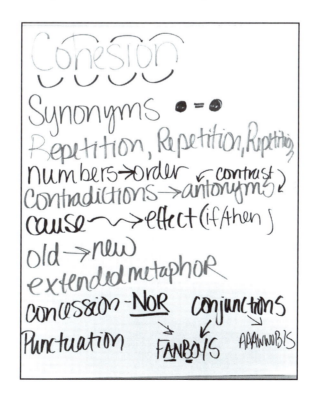

SHORT WRITING AND REVISION STRATEGIES

## Make It Better

A fun way to test if their cohesion connectors are strong and clear is to have students cut their writing into sentences. For longer pieces, they can cut paragraphs apart. Each student places their pieces in an envelope and trades with another student. The partners should be able to easily place the pieces in order. If a partner gets the order wrong or is struggling with it, the writer needs to make the connections between ideas clearer.

## Make It Happen with Any Text

This strategy works well with any genre of text, but the techniques may differ in a narrative text versus an informational text.

## Make It Happen at Any Level

| Emerging Readers and Writers (K–2) | Experienced Readers and Writers (6–12) |
|---|---|
| Using pages from a wordless picture book, ask students to put the images in order. This can help students practice sequencing skills and looking at details within the images to make connections. | Take a complex text and cut it into sentences or sections. Ask students to unscramble the writing and discuss how the author created cohesion in their writing. |

# PART 3: FEEDBACK AND ASSESSMENT

# FEEDBACK WITH AN IMPACT

I think many of us can recall a time when a teacher's comments on a paper were less than encouraging. A paper bleeding with red ink and brief comments like "awk" or "more here" does not do much to help writers. I sobbed over an A– on a poem where my teacher's only unhelpful note was a single, circled word with *WC* scrawled on top of it.

Dear reader, if you too are confused by that note, it meant she did not like my *Word Choice*. When I asked her about it after class, and tried to defend my wording, she replied, "If you have to explain it, it isn't very good."

I was crushed. I have never forgotten that poem or that teacher's note.

When I got into my own classroom, grading haunted me. My least favorite day of the school year was the day students' large research papers were due. Every year, the weeks that followed that due date were a constant fog of grading and guilt. I took those papers everywhere—to coffee shops, on airplanes, to the doctor's office, even to a baseball game—just in case the grading bug hit. It never did. The tote bag of papers, however, got to go on a lot of field trips.

Eventually, I graded all those research papers and passed them back. But for all the time and effort that I put into the comments on students' writing, they barely looked at my notations. I would find those carefully graded papers wedged under desks or left on the floor the day I handed them back.

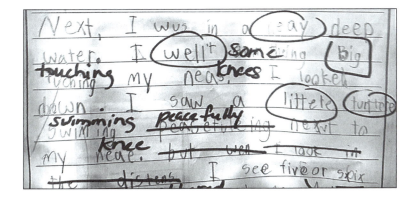

**Feedback that doesn't encourage the writer.**

97

# Effective Feedback

What I experienced as a student and later as a teacher around grading and feedback illustrates what we now know about effective feedback. To be most effective, feedback should be timely, specific, and actionable (Fisher, Frey, and Hattie 2016; Hattie and Clarke 2019; Schmoker 2018). The feedback from my English teacher was not actionable or helpful. The feedback I provided my own students was not timely. In both cases, the teacher notes did not lead to better student writing. Given the time and energy teachers spend providing feedback, we need to think about the impact our feedback has on student writers. Is the feedback likely to help improve a writer's skills or just fix one piece of writing? Are the notes we make in the margins timely, specific, and actionable?

## Timely

One of the benefits of short reading and writing is that the process creates a space for immediate feedback. Students crave feedback, especially on their writing. Walk into a class of second grade writers and you will see nothing but waving hands and students pleading, "Can you read this?" Even older writers, who might not plead with you to read every sentence, appreciate the smile, the nod, and the whispered "Oh, I like this!" when someone reads their work.

According to Mike Schmoker's *Focus*, "Lessons built around same-day formative assessment or checks for understanding produce student learning effects that are 'among the largest ever reported'" (Schmoker 2018, 70, quoting Black and Wiliam 1998, 61). Same-day feedback ensures that students are still attuned to what they wrote and why; if a student cannot remember writing something, they won't care to correct it.

When students are writing only a few sentences, I can often get to every student, reading their responses and providing feedback on the spot. In the case that students' short writing pieces come home with me, I can provide feedback on them much more quickly than on a stack of long papers.

## Specific

In addition to helping ensure feedback is timely, using short reading and writing tasks helps teachers provide specific, pointed feedback. When giving feedback on only a few sentences, we can focus on the skill students are learning and practicing in the moment. The target skill (such as using evidence, writing a main idea, or even crafting a complete sentence) is the only thing we should be commenting on. This precise and targeted "feedback is most effective when goals are specific and challenging but when task complexity is low" (Kluger and DeNisi 1996, as cited in Hattie and Clarke 2019, 4).

Even when we assign short reading and writing tasks, we may still need to stifle the urge to correct everything. Matthew Johnson, author of *Flash Feedback* (2020), calls this kind of feedback *over-response*. "When teachers comment on every passing thought and observation as they work through a paper, they are more likely to confuse or scare students away from learning any of [the many skills]" (20). If we focus on one key skill or concept, we help students focus on it as well and support their growth as readers and writers.

## Actionable

Feedback, to be actionable, must come before the final draft. According to Johnson, feedback received after a writer has completed the writing is an autopsy, not a path forward (2020). If we want students to be better writers and more willing to revise, our feedback should provide them with the time and place to do so. Providing specific feedback in the initial stages of the writing process makes that feedback more actionable.

The *most* actionable feedback is when we help students see the need themselves. If I circle a word that was used incorrectly (think *to* when it should be *too*), then the student merely makes my correction. If I design learning so students return to their writing looking for misused words, and they make their own changes or revisions, they are more likely to remember their learning.

With any kind of revision, I ask students to compare the new version to the original and talk about the change. How did the writing improve? Reflecting on how a specific technique or strategy improved the writing is an important last step to transferring the skill. Fisher, Frey, and Hattie note that when students reflect on their own strategic thinking and action, they become aware of "internal scripts" they can follow in the future (2016, 101).

More broadly, sharing the changes we make to our writing—removing a word, adjusting a sentence, adding a detail—illustrates that revision and editing are beneficial acts that improve every student's writing. Refining a piece after we write it doesn't have to be hard or daunting; it can be as simple as one small change.

Becoming a stronger reader and writer starts one sentence at a time. And when we can provide fast feedback and encouragement for even one sentence, it often leads the student to write the next one. Teresa Amabile and Steven Kramer studied creative professionals and found that "everyday progress—even a small win—can make all the difference in how they feel and perform" (2011, para. 3). Amabile and Kramer's research on how feedback spurs adults' progress and happiness at work gives us insights into the feelings students have as they work in our classrooms.

## Motivation and Progress

Effective feedback feeds an important emotion: motivation. For students who are building confidence and competency in literacy skills, being a "good" reader or writer often seems like a hazy goal in the distance. Think of it like an abandoned New Year's resolution: Running a marathon sounds good on January 1st, but by February, you may have given up. It is hard to see the individual steps needed to get to the finish line.

We all want to feel the thrill of a win. Research scientist Jude King notes, "Without the small wins, the big one likely won't happen—we give up in disappointment and frustration before we get to the big win. The small wins hold the key to momentum" (2019, para. 8). In business and in the classroom, "every achievement—big or small—activates our brain's reward circuitry… which leaves us feeling energized, confident and motivated" (2019, para. 6).

When we provide timely feedback to students, they are more likely to leave our classrooms with a clear picture about the work they are doing and the progress they made. Seeing progress toward a goal means they will be more likely to read and write again tomorrow. Becoming a better reader and writer can be a slow process. Students need encouragement to keep going. The feedback that we provide is critical in that process.

| Good Feedback Provides Students | Good Assessment Provides Teachers |
|---|---|
| → Reinforcement that they are on the right track<br>→ A sense of accomplishment<br>→ Actionable next steps<br>→ Progress toward the goal of being a better reader and writer | → Input for your next mini-lesson or skill<br>→ Understanding of precisely where students are struggling<br>→ Awareness about who needs more intensive support<br>→ Progress toward the goal of creating better readers and writers |

Many of the strategies in this section are directed at providing feedback on writing, and it may seem like reading feedback has been shortchanged. However, keep in mind that writing about reading is an effective measure of reading comprehension. According to Lemov, Driggs, and Woolway, "Writing makes thinking permanent; it allows teachers to assess effectively to check for understanding" (2016, 97). In-class quick writes can be used for assessment and feedback for either reading or writing.

The small assessment strategies described below aim to provide teachers with immediate data on student understanding of content. They will also provide critical feedback to students to keep them motivated to persevere during the hard work of reading and writing.

# SHORT FEEDBACK STRATEGIES

For short reading and short writing tasks, we need quick ways to provide feedback, assessment, and yes, even grades. I use a combination of the following strategies (listed from least to most formal) to check for understanding, guide my instruction, provide specific next steps, and give students small wins. Whether I score short assignments and include them as part of students' grades depends on the time of the year, students' overall understanding of the text or task, and the amount of class time spent on the task. Often, the feedback provided is part of the learning journey, with no grade attached.

## Walk and Talk

Short reading and writing moments allow me to work my way around the room looking over students' shoulders to see where they are excelling and struggling. If students are annotating text, I can see what they are marking, and more importantly, what they may be missing. I often walk from desk to desk with a clipboard and a copy of my seating chart. In addition to providing feedback, clarifying misconceptions, and gaining insights that will inform my next instructional steps, I make notes on who I have seen and how their work is going.

Walk and Talk provides valuable time for learning conversations. Without the entire class watching, I can kneel down next to a student for a conversation about their writing. I can nudge an early finisher to extend their writing, reassure a reluctant writer that they are on the right path, support a student trying something new, and provide clarity to a student who is off track.

Walking and talking to listen to and watch students can be a highly effective means of formative assessment: "Even one to two minutes of circulating can give you an adequate idea of student progress" (Schmoker 2018, 59). The key is that this feedback is *in the moment.* I didn't always have time to see every student every day. However, I tried to make the moments count, and if I wasn't going to grade the assignments, it was even less critical to see every student every time.

SHORT FEEDBACK STRATEGIES

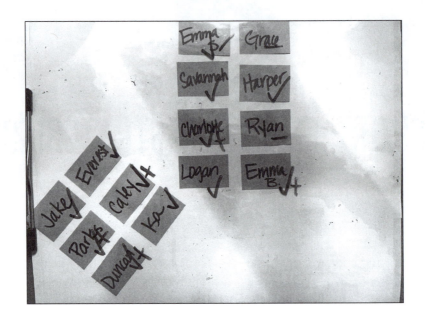

## Pair and Share

Pair and Share works well for giving and getting feedback, and also for providing a few extra moments to confer with a student or prepare the next activity. To keep Pair and Share from getting out of hand, make sure students have something written before they get into pairs, and provide only a brief amount of time for the share. When it's time for the whole class to reassemble, I give students a countdown. This both honors and gives students time to complete the real conversations that may be happening.

After the class has reassembled, extend this activity by asking someone to "share something they liked or learned from their partner." I have never seen a student beam more than when a peer tells them their writing is good enough to share.

## Check and Go

Sometimes, teachers need to know where students are in their understanding before moving on to the next step, the next page, or the next skill. Check and Go is a more systematic version of Walk and Talk. I ask a question or provide a prompt and make sure I get an answer from everyone. I walk the room on a mission: to see every response before we move on. I often had a stamp in my hand, using it to mark students' work as I went. This helped me know which

SHORT FEEDBACK STRATEGIES

students I had seen. I will also add that students, no matter the age, universally want that stamp. They will wave you over to read their answer to get it.

Often, you'll know exactly which responses you need to spend an extra moment or two looking at closely. For many prompts, seeing a couple key words is enough to know that a student is on the right track. I can walk the room quickly to read over responses and provide one of four check marks. Students get a quick bit of feedback, and converting the check marks into grades is simple to do if needed.

**Check and Go Scoring Sample** (See page 120 for a printable version designed for sticky notes.)

| ✔+ | Response shows understanding of the task.—Full credit (10/10) |
|---|---|
| ✔ | Response shows an attempt but may be missing elements.—Partial credit (8/10) |
| ✔- | Response is off track and shows confusion over the topic.—Half credit (5/10) |
| — | No response, *yet.* I always return to see if they have written something later. (0/10) |

## Pile and Grade

When students turn in a piece of short writing, such as a summary of a text or an analysis of ideas we have read, my goal is to spend a minimal amount of time giving them feedback. Pile and Grade works nicely for quick assessment of short writing. Start by creating a basic rubric for each of the four possible scores. I made a sticky note for each of the four options to make my work easy. I then placed the sticky notes on the desk in a row.

### Sample Pile and Grade Categories

| High Scores | | Low Scores | |
|---|---|---|---|
| 4 | 3 | 2 | 1 |
| Great response. No notes. | Solid response. One note of clarification or correction. | Some areas of strength and some areas to improve. | Valiant attempt, but missing key components. |

© Shell Education

136447—Short Texts, Big Impact **103**

SHORT FEEDBACK STRATEGIES

Handling each student's response only once, and making no notes, make two choices. First, decide if the response belongs in the High Scores or Low Scores category. Then decide which score it gets within that category. Place the student's paper below the sticky note with the score you have assigned. Continue in this manner, making a pile below each of the four sticky notes.

When finished, you have quickly assigned students one of four scores. If needed, you can decide what those scores are worth on a traditional grading scale. You may also find that some responses are between the scores and deserve an additional half point. It is your classroom; do what makes sense.

What made this method work for me is the time I saved by not agonizing about every single score point. Not writing on every student's work also kept this feedback method quick. I often provided clear feedback for improvement to those students who earned a "1," but that stack was usually small. You might opt to pull students in a category into a small group to provide targeted support.

One note from my classroom: If a student tried, they got points. If they didn't doodle a monster, they got credit for an attempt. (Unless the monster was really cool and had a name. Then maybe they got half-credit.)

## The Short Rubric

The most robust scoring tool is a short rubric. A rubric defines the criteria to be scored, the levels of quality for each criteria, and the ratings (or scores) for each level.

Rubrics require a bit of work on the front end. I have written some overly complicated rubrics that I fully regretted by the time I had scored four or five papers. When designing a rubric, there are a few key things to keep in mind:

- Rubrics are best when they are written in kid-friendly language. That doesn't mean scoring in emojis. Using the academic terms for criteria helps students understand the skill and the score.

- Rubrics should only score skills and concepts you have taught or reviewed. And when it comes to grammar and mechanics skills, asking students to have mastered every single convention in the English language is a fool's errand. As much as you might want to mark every single one of those errors, ask yourself how it benefits students.

- Make sure there is a balance between content and mechanics, and keep in mind the balance need not be 50/50. There are very few times in our lives where a typo or a misspelled word matters as much as the content of our writing or thinking. Consider building rubrics that value content more than mechanics.

- Rubrics with four score levels (instead of three or five) require graders to determine if something is high or low. When the rubric has a middle score, we tend to use it by default.

- Consider cocreating rubrics with students. Provide a framework of the general structure and categories, and spend time together as a class writing the description.

SHORT FEEDBACK STRATEGIES

*Teacher Talk:* *What does a 3 look like for text evidence? How is that different from a 4?*

- I love a rubric that fits on a sticky note! See page 120 for a printable rubric designed for a 3x3 sticky note. To use it, print the rubric. Next, cover each of the squares with a 3x3 sticky note. Then, place the paper with the sticky notes on it back into your printer and reprint the template again on the sticky notes.

- The sample rubric shown here, for an evidence-based response to reading, incorporates some of the principles mentioned above. Using rubrics like this helps us clearly see where each student needs specific support. I could easily form writing small groups based on students' scores in each individual category.

## Sample Short Reading Response Rubric (Grades 3 and up)

| Category | 4 | 3 | 2 | 1 |
|---|---|---|---|---|
| **Clear Answer to Prompt** | Clear and correct response | Correct response | Unclear response | Incorrect response |
| **Text Evidence Supports the Answer** | Well-chosen evidence that is clearly explained | Evidence may lack explanation or clarity | Evidence is present, but is not clearly connected to answer | No evidence provided |
| **Mechanics: Sentence Structure** | Uses complete sentences with capital letters and end punctuation | Writing may contain run-ons or fragments, but with punctuation and capitalization | Writing contains run-ons and/or sentence fragments | No sentence boundaries, punctuation, or capitalization |

© Shell Education

136447—Short Texts, Big Impact **105**

# APPENDIXES

## A. Sample Short Texts
- What's Right at All Costs
- The Mystery of the Beeswax Wreck
- Ever American
- Homework: Helpful or Harmful?

## B. Sample Anchor Charts
- Choices Authors Make
- What Can We Delete?
- Crafting Cohesion
- SCAMPER
- Author's Craft
- Unstuck List

## C. Teacher Resources
- Short Text Lesson Planner
- Text-Dependent Writing Prompts
- Printable Rubrics

## D. Activity Pages
- Roll a Response
- Roll a Revision
- Evidence Battle
- Storyboard

# Untold Stories: José Arturo Castellanos Contreras

## What's Right at All Costs

In 1893, a hero was born in El Salvador. He grew up to save 40,000 **Jewish** people from the Nazi concentration camps of Europe. But he did not see what he did as heroic. He saw a friend in danger and did what he could to save him. This hero's name is José Arturo Castellanos Contreras.

Castellanos was born into a military family. His father was a general. When he was 16 years old, he was sent to military school. He spent 26 years in the army. He became the **consulate general** in Germany. His job was to issue **visas** and renew passports. Little did he know how important his job would become.

In Germany, the rising Nazi forces took to the streets. Over two nights, 30,000 Jewish men were arrested and sent to concentration camps. The Nazis torched **synagogues**. Jewish homes and business were vandalized. People were beaten in public. Close to one hundred Jewish people were killed.

Castellanos was shocked. He wrote his government. He requested visas for people wanting to flee Europe. The government said no. Instead, they sent him to Switzerland.

There, Castellanos met a Jewish businessman named György Mandl. They became friends. Mandl had escaped from the Nazis. But Switzerland had strict **immigration** laws. Mandl was afraid of being deported. If caught, he would be sent to a concentration camp.

Castellanos was worried for Mandl. He wrote his government again. He asked for a visa for his friend. Again, the answer was no.

Afraid for Mandl's life, Castellanos decided to **forge** the documents. These fake papers made Mandl a citizen of El Salvador. They also changed his name to George Mantello.

Castellanos decided he could help other Jewish people, too. The fake documents were easy to create. He hired college students as typists. They all worked together to re-create the same fake papers that saved Mandl's life. The team created thousands of these documents. They were sent across Europe to other Jewish people living in danger. In all, 40,000 people were saved!

In 1944, Castellanos asked El Salvador to recognize these fake documents and grant protections to the Jewish people. This time, the government said yes.

—*David Scott*

Source: *Untold Stories* © 2022 Teacher Created Materials

APPENDIX A: SAMPLE SHORT TEXTS

**LESSON 22**

# The Mystery of the Beeswax Wreck

Ahh, ancient galleons, shipwrecks, and buried treasure! Stories of adventure in the high seas are irresistible. They are especially exciting when they are true. This is the case with a ship that sank off the coast of Manzanita, Oregon. People have been debating its origins for over 200 years.

The oldest chapter of this mysterious shipwreck story surfaced in the journal of a fur trader. In 1813, Alexander Henry wrote that a group of Clatsop Indians arrived at the trading post with blocks of beeswax. This savvy trader knew that honeybees were not native to the region, and so the beeswax must have come from far away. He inquired about it. The Native Americans shared with him the story of a nearby wrecked ship.

Some have speculated the ship was from Japan. Others said it was from Portugal or England. It is rumored that some sailors swam ashore and buried chests of treasure on Neahkahnie Mountain. For decades adventurers have searched for both the sunken wreck and the buried treasure. Some individuals have pursued the mystery for years.

Roughly 70 years ago, an eight-year-old beachcomber discovered bits of Chinese pottery on the beach. Scientists dated these precious pieces from the 1500s. They believe they came from the shipwreck. But just because the pottery came from China doesn't mean the sunken ship did. Other artifacts found in the area date from the same time period. Over the years, people have recovered teak timbers and stoneware vessels for beer, wine, water, and perfume.

Fortunately, the Spanish kept detailed shipping logs from the 1500s. Historians now believe the ship in question was the Santo Cristo de Burgos. The ship left Manila in the Philippines laden with goods to trade. It was bound for Mexico and its silver. Experts believe the ship and its crew suffered from navigation problems. They lost their way in a storm and overshot their destination. The ship hit trouble on the open sea and sank along the Oregon coast.

Today, a volunteer group called the Beeswax Wreck Research Project is conducting an offshore survey. The team is made up of students, archeologists, and historians. Using sonar and an oversized metal detector, the searchers hope to find the sunken galleon. They want to solve the mystery of the earliest shipwreck in the Pacific Northwest.

Two men bring a large block of beeswax in from the water.

Underwater cameras are used to investigate the wreckage.

Source: *Focused Reading—Student Guided Practice Book* © 2014 Teacher Created Materials

## Ever American

### Huda Essa

"But where are you *really* from?" the boy asked young Huda Essa. She and her friends said they were from Dearborn, Michigan. He only asked Essa this question. People never asked her friends this question. Essa looked a little different from her friends. Her skin and hair were darker than theirs were.

Essa had always lived in America. Yet it seemed to her that she was not a *normal* American. She learned this from school, books, and TV. Americans portrayed there did not look like her family. They did not pray like her or eat the foods she ate. Most of those Americans only spoke English.

Essa tried to fit in by changing things about herself. She would not speak her home language in front of others. When her hair became curly, she styled it straight. She even tried to change her name.

She later wondered what it meant to be an American. Soon after, she visited Palestine. This was her family's country of **origin**. Their home language, foods, and **customs** were normal there. Essa learned that her other **culture** was wonderful. This helped her become proud of her **Muslim** and Arab **identities**.

Her trip also helped her know that she *is* an American. An American is anyone whose home is in America. It is not a language, skin color, name, or religion. It belongs to **native** people and people with origins from all over the world.

Essa did not want anyone to feel like she once did. She chose to become a teacher. She taught students to respect themselves and all others.

One way they did this was through sharing name stories. Essa wanted everyone to learn from name stories. She wrote a book, *Teach Us Your Name*. She also wrote a speech called "Your Name Is the Key!"

Essa still works toward her goals. She wants every person to feel included and loved. She writes and speaks about this to help people around the world.

—*Huda Essa*

Source: *Untold Stories* © 2022 Teacher Created Materials

APPENDIX A: SAMPLE SHORT TEXTS

# HOMEWORK: HELPFUL OR HARMFUL?

**LESSON 17**

For generations, homework has been a controversial topic, and it continues to be. Most kids hate doing it, many parents are frustrated by it, and nearly all teachers are tired of grading it.

You may be surprised to learn there is little scientific evidence that shows homework makes kids smarter. And there is only minimal research showing that high school students who complete homework regularly do better on test scores. Yet most teachers continue to dole out daily assignments. And so, the controversy continues.

Homework proponents claim that both the school day and the school year are too short for all the learning students need to do. They say homework creates a connection between school and home. It gives families something to work on together. Completing homework regularly helps students develop time-management and organizational skills. It helps kids hone healthy work habits. Additionally, kids need more time to practice reading and writing. Most kids need extra time studying math facts and content-area vocabulary. Homework reinforces these types of skills. Working at home also allows students focused quiet time away from the distractions of their peers and a busy classroom.

Homework opponents argue there is scarcely any academic value to homework. They say homework creates unnecessary pressure and stress. They argue it is unhealthy for students and families. Some say that it interferes with family life and community involvement. Plus, those students without support at home may flounder without teacher guidance. This will lead to more frustration and a higher risk of failure. Opponents argue there is much for students to explore and learn outside the world of traditional schooling. They think children need the freedom to play sports, pursue hobbies, and enjoy downtime with friends and family.

Where will this debate end? Will it end? Is there a middle ground to be found? Would students be happier to complete homework if they designed their own homework? Could teachers give homework less frequently and find ways to make it more enticing and enjoyable? What do you think? Where do you stand on this great debate?

Source: *Focused Reading—Student Guided Practice Book* © 2014 Teacher Created Materials

APPENDIX B: SAMPLE ANCHOR CHARTS

## ANCHOR CHART: CHOICES AUTHORS MAKE

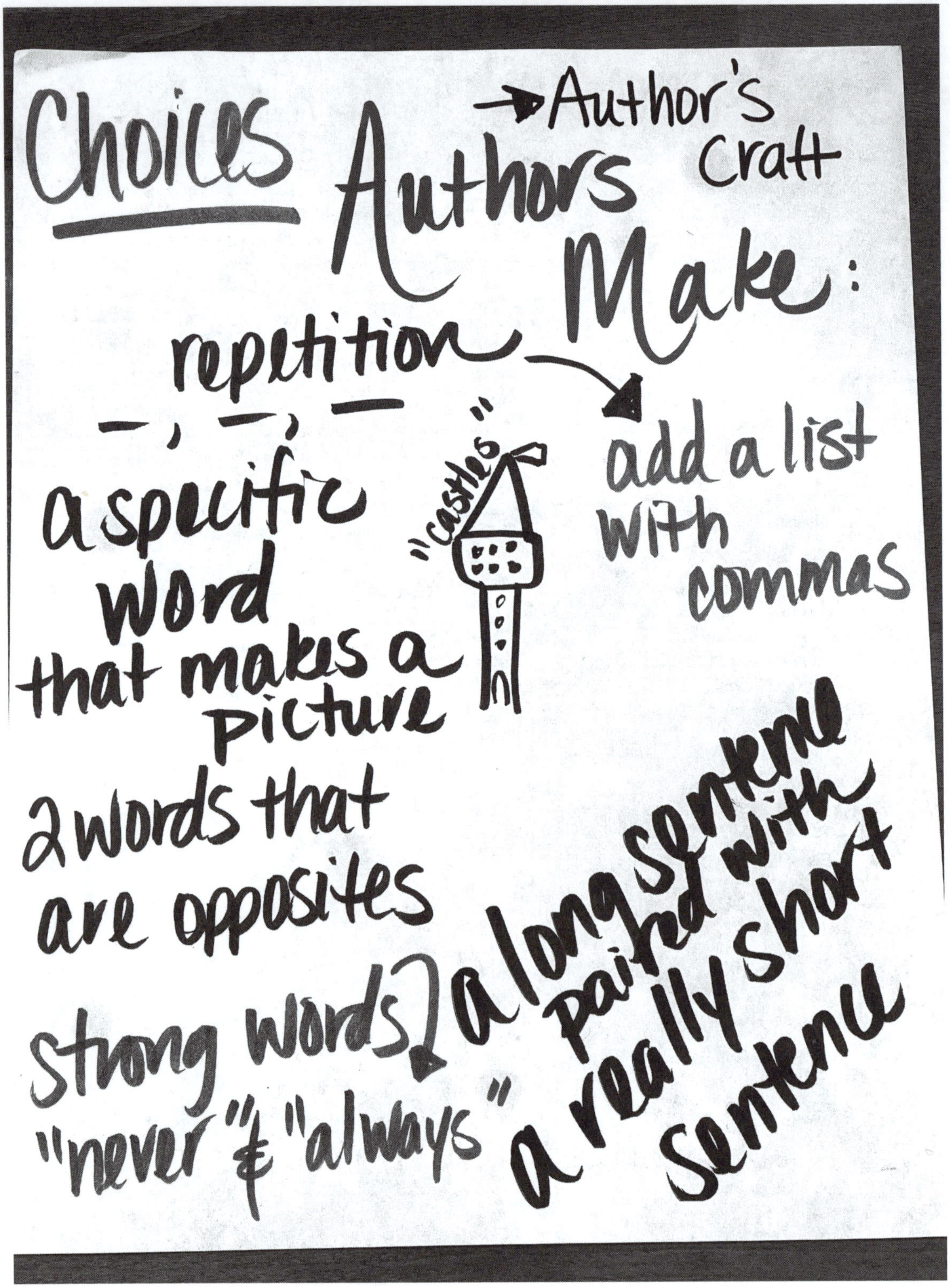

Choices Authors → Author's Craft Make:

repetition

—, —, —

a specific word that makes a picture

"castles"

add a list with commas

2 words that are opposites

strong words? "never" & "always"

a long sentence paired with a really short sentence

112    136447—Short Texts, Big Impact

© Shell Education

APPENDIX B: SAMPLE ANCHOR CHARTS

## ANCHOR CHART: WHAT CAN WE DELETE?

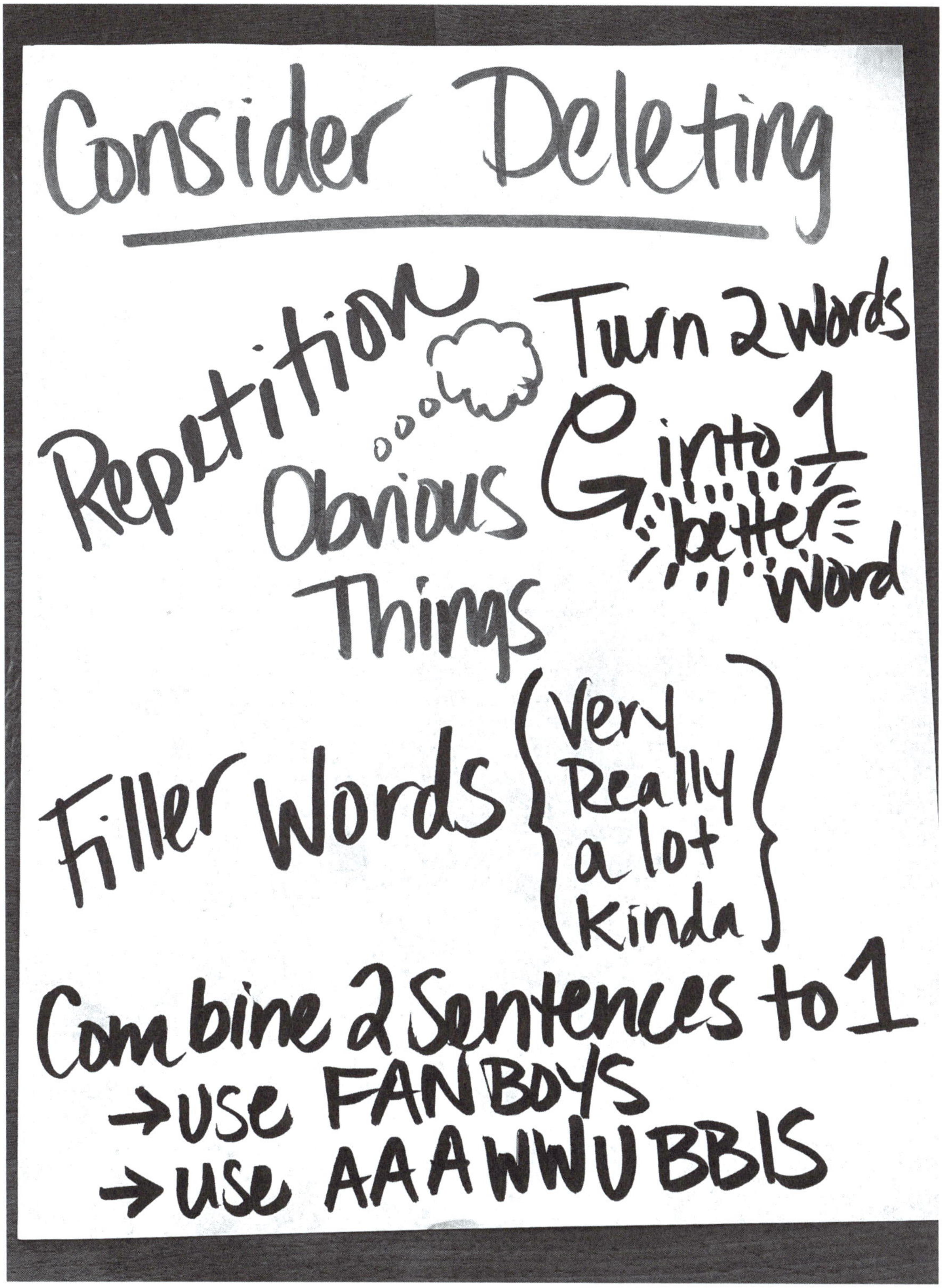

# Consider Deleting

Repetition

Obvious Things

Turn 2 words
6 into 1
better word

Filler Words { Very Really a lot Kinda }

Combine 2 Sentences to 1
→ Use FANBOYS
→ Use AAAWWUBBIS

© Shell Education

136447—Short Texts, Big Impact  **113**

APPENDIX B: SAMPLE ANCHOR CHARTS

## ANCHOR CHART: CRAFTING COHESION

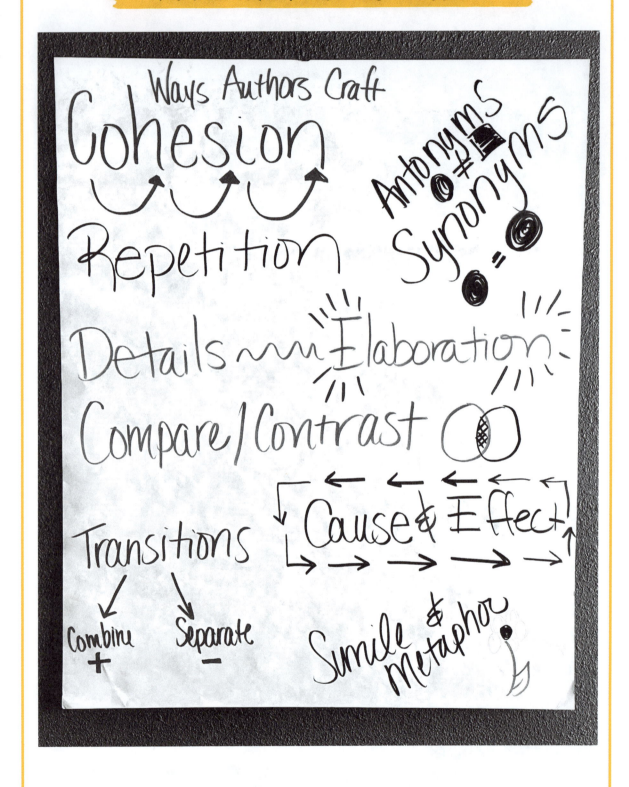

APPENDIX B: SAMPLE ANCHOR CHARTS

## ANCHOR CHART: SCAMPER

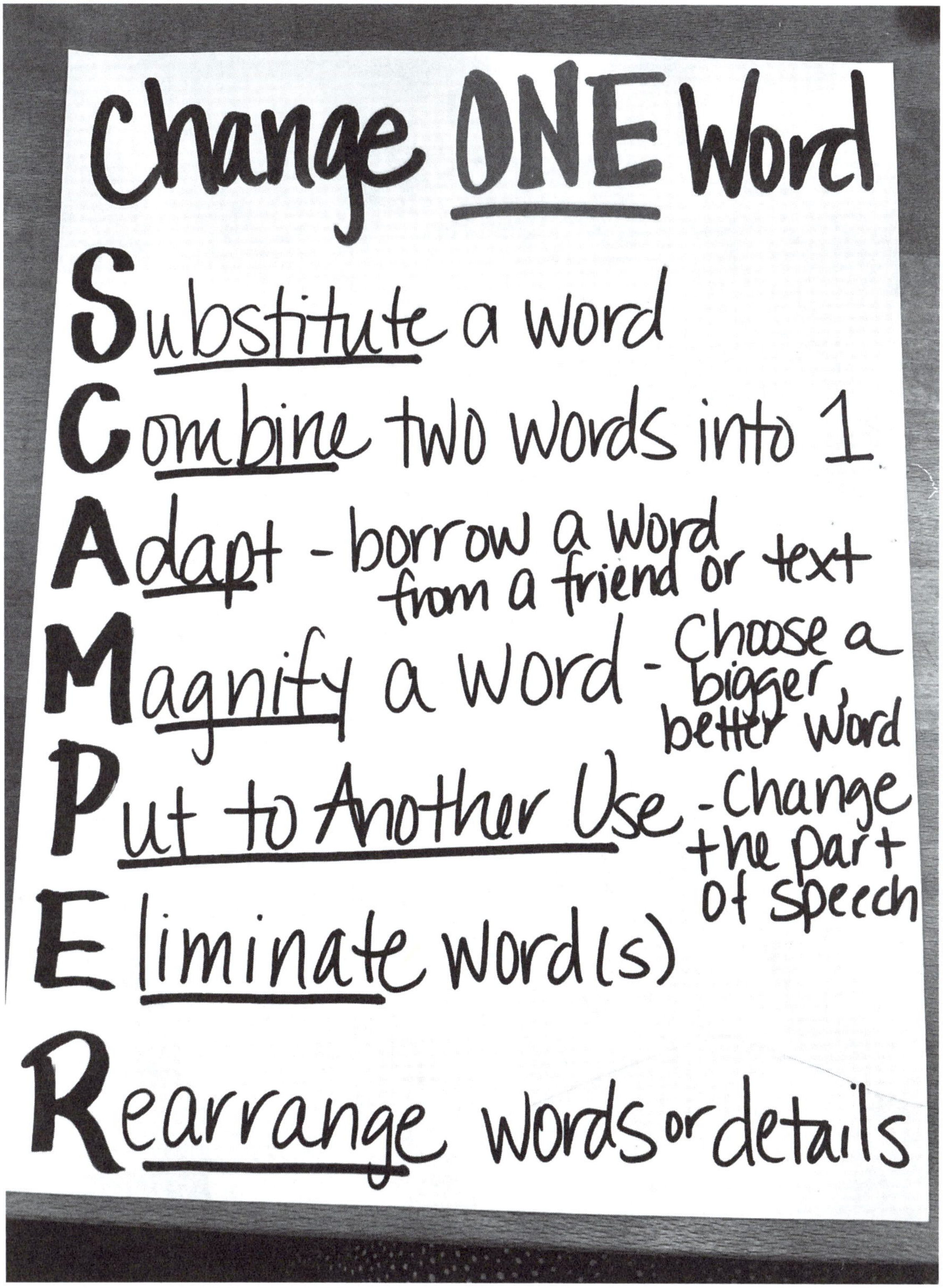

# Change ONE Word

**S**ubstitute a word

**C**ombine two words into 1.

**A**dapt - borrow a word from a friend or text

**M**agnify a Word - Choose a bigger, better word

**P**ut to Another Use - Change the part of speech

**E**liminate word(s)

**R**earrange words or details

© Shell Education

136447—Short Texts, Big Impact **115**

APPENDIX B: SAMPLE ANCHOR CHARTS

## ANCHOR CHART: AUTHOR'S CRAFT

# Author's Craft

**What** is the author doing?

**Why** is the author doing it?

**How** can you use this in your writing?

APPENDIX B: SAMPLE ANCHOR CHARTS

## ANCHOR CHART: UNSTUCK LIST

**Stuck? Try This!**

It starts with …
In the end …
If ___ then ___ } FANBOYS
Despite …
Just like …  Or Try AAWWUBBIS
Depending on …
In addition to …

© Shell Education

136447—Short Texts, Big Impact **117**

APPENDIX C: TEACHER RESOURCES

## Short Text Lesson Planner

**Short Text Title:**

| Skill Focus | Activity/Prompt/Question |
|---|---|
| **Vocabulary:** | |
| | |
| **Reading:** | |
| | |
| **Writing:** | |
| | |
| **Revision and Grammar:** | |
| | |
| **How will students show mastery?** | |

**118**  136447—Short Texts, Big Impact

© Shell Education

APPENDIX C: TEACHER RESOURCES

# Text-Dependent Writing Prompts

Explain why (*item/object*) is important in the text. Use evidence from the text to support your answer.

Explain your opinion about why we should or should not (*two-sided issue*). Use evidence from the text to support your answer.

Explain how the (*narrator/speaker/poet's*) feelings about (*person/event*) change. Use evidence from the text to support your answer.

Explain how (*character*) shows (*trait*) throughout the story. Use evidence from the text to support your answer.

Explain how (*item/development/change*) has affected (*group of people*). Use evidence from the text to support your answer.

Explain how the author develops the idea of (*main idea*) in the article. Use evidence from the text to support your answer.

Explain how (*plot point*) contributes to the development of the theme. Use evidence from the text to support your answer.

Explain how (*event/item*) changes (*character*). Use evidence from the text to support your answer.

Explain how (*item/advancement*) (*benefitted/affected/changed*) (*group of people*). Use evidence from the text to support your answer.

© Shell Education

136447—Short Texts, Big Impact **119**

APPENDIX C: TEACHER RESOURCES                                        FOR USE WITH PAGE 105

# Printable Rubrics

## Quick Write Quick Grade

 **Well Done:** Thoughtful response that includes all the components.

 **Solid Start:** Great start. Missing an element or polish.

 **Off Track:** Revisit your writing. Check your response for errors.

— **No Response *Yet.*** Give it a try!

## Quick Write Quick Grade

 **Well Done:** Thoughtful response that includes all the components.

 **Solid Start:** Great start. Missing an element or polish.

 **Off Track:** Revisit your writing. Check your response for errors.

— **No Response *Yet.*** Give it a try!

## Quick Write Quick Grade

 **Well Done:** Thoughtful response that includes all the components.

 **Solid Start:** Great start. Missing an element or polish.

 **Off Track:** Revisit your writing. Check your response for errors.

— **No Response *Yet.*** Give it a try!

## Quick Write Quick Grade

 **Well Done:** Thoughtful response that includes all the components.

 **Solid Start:** Great start. Missing an element or polish.

 **Off Track:** Revisit your writing. Check your response for errors.

— **No Response *Yet.*** Give it a try!

FOR USE WITH PAGE 41

Name _____ Date _____

# ROLL A RESPONSE

**Directions:** Roll the number cube to determine how you will respond to the text. Craft your answer on a sticky note.

| | |
|---|---|
| ⚀ | **What is the main idea of the text? Support your answer.** |
| ⚁ | **How does the information in the text compare to what you have read/heard before?** |
| ⚂ | **Find a tricky paragraph/section of the text. Rewrite it to make it simpler.** |
| ⚃ | **Summarize the text.** |
| ⚄ | **What do you learn from the text features? How do the text features help the text?** |
| ⚅ | **What is the author's perspective/attitude toward the topic? Support your answer with evidence.** |

© Shell Education

136447—Short Texts, Big Impact **121**

FOR USE WITH PAGE 90

Name _____ Date _____

## ROLL A REVISION

**Directions:** Roll the number cube to determine how you will revise your writing. Craft your revision on a sticky note.

| | |
|---|---|
|  ⚀ | **Choose a sentence and simplify it into three words.** |
|  ⚁ | **Choose a sentence and expand it with details and description to make it twice as long.** |
|  ⚂ | **Choose a sentence and move it to a new place.** |
|  ⚃ | **Find a place to add a piece of figurative language. (Try simile, metaphor, or personification.)** |
|  ⚄ | **Find a scratchy section that you don't love yet. Work on it to make it stronger.** |
|  ⚅ | **Revise a sentence to start with a subordinating conjunction. (Use an AAAWWUBBIS word.)** |

**122** 136447—Short Texts, Big Impact

© Shell Education

Name _____ Date _____

# EVIDENCE BATTLE

**Directions:** Write your best text evidence on a sticky note. Work with your group to determine the overall best text evidence.

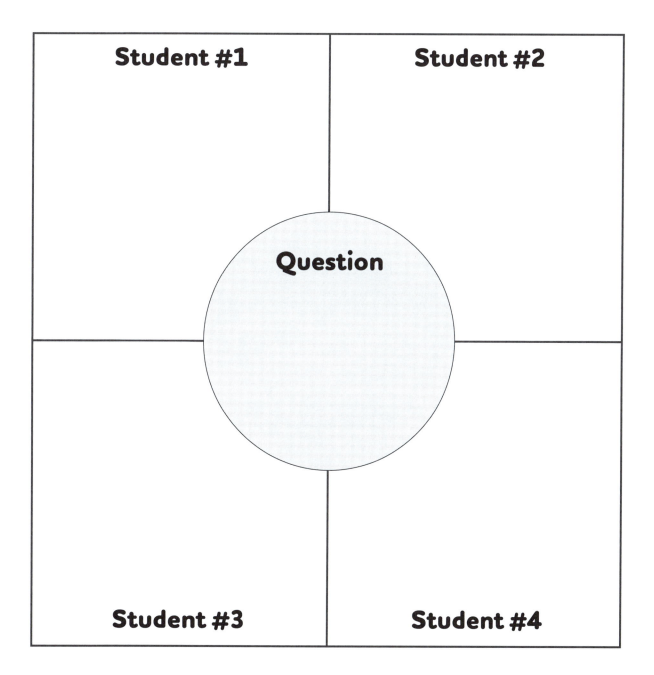

136447—Short Texts, Big Impact

**Name** _____ **Date** _____

## STORYBOARD

**Directions:** Sketch the story events on sticky notes. Place them on the panels. Share your draft with a partner. Revise your story as much as you wish until you are ready to write it.

**My title:** _____

| | | |
|---|---|---|
| 1. | 2. | 3. |
| 4. | 5. | 6. |

FOR USE WITH PAGE 79

# REFERENCES

Allen, Janet. 1999. *Words, Words, Words: Teaching Vocabulary in Grades 4–12*. Routledge.

Amabile, Teresa. M., and Steven. J. Kramer. 2011. "The Power of Small Wins." *Harvard Business Review*. hbr.org/2011/05/the-power-of-small-wins.

Anderson, Jeff. 2005. *Mechanically Inclined: Building Grammar, Usage, and Style into Writer's Workshop*. Stenhouse.

Anderson, Jeff. 2007. *Everyday Editing*. Stenhouse.

Anderson, Jeff. 2011. *10 Things Every Writer Needs to Know*. Stenhouse.

Anderson, Jeff, and Deborah Dean. 2014. *Revision Decisions: Talking Through Sentences and Beyond*. Stenhouse.

Black, Paul, and Dylan Wiliam. 1998. "Assessment and Classroom Learning." *Assessment in Education: Principles, Policy and Practice* 5 (1): 7–74. doi.org/10.1080/0969595980050102.

Bogard, Jennifer M., and Mary C. McMackin. 2015. *Writing Is Magic, or Is It? Using the Mentor Text to Develop the Writer's Craft*. Shell Education.

Bruffee, Kenneth A. 1972. *A Short Course in Writing: Composition, Collaborative Learning, and Constructive Reading*. Winthrop Publishers.

Braddock, Richard Reed., Richard Lloyd-Jones, and Lowell A. Schoer. 1963. *Research in Written Composition*. National Council of Teachers of English.

Cappello, Marva, and Nancy T. Walker. 2020. *Get the Picture: Visual Literacy in Content-Area Instruction*. Shell Education.

Carroll, Joyce Armstrong. 1991. "Drawing into Meaning: A Powerful Writing Tool." *English Journal* 80 (6): 34–38. doi.org/10.58680/ej19918252.

Carroll, Joyce Armstrong. 2007. *Authentic Strategies for High Stakes Tests: A Practical Guide for English Language Arts*. Absey and Co.

Carroll, Joyce Armstrong. 2011. *Ratiocination: Weaving the Threads of Grammar, Revision, and Editing*. Absey and Co.

Carroll, Joyce Armstrong, and Edward E. Wilson. 2012. *Four by Four: Practical Methods for Writing Persuasively*. Libraries Unlimited.

Carroll, Joyce Armstrong, and Edward E. Wilson. 2019. *Acts of Teaching: How to Teach Writing: A Text, a Reader, a Narrative,* third edition. Libraries Unlimited.

Clear, James. 2018. *Atomic Habits: An Easy and Proven Way to Build Good Habits and Break Bad Ones*. Avery Books.

Cook, Ann. 2000. *American Accent Training: A Guide to Speaking and Pronouncing American English for Everyone Who Speaks English as a Second Language*, second edition. Barron's.

Davis, Thankful D., Katie Schrodt, and Sungyoon Lee. 2024. "An Exploration of the Impact of Quality Illustrations in Children's Picture Books on Preschool Student Narrative Ability." *Reading Psychology* 45 (7): 639–661. doi:10.1080/02702711.2024.2351480.

# REFERENCES

Deak, JoAnn M. 2010. *Your Fantastic Elastic Brain: Stretch It, Shape It*. Illustrated by Sarah Ackerley. Little Pickle Press.

Dean, Ceri B., Elizabeth Ross Hubbell, Howard Pitler, and Bj Stone. 2012. *Classroom Instruction That Works: Research-Based Strategies for Increasing Student Achievement*, second edition. ASCD.

Eberle, Bob. 1971. *Scamper: Creative Games and Activities for Imagination Development*. D. O. K. Publishing.

Elbow, Peter. 1998. *Writing with Power: Techniques for Mastering the Writing Process*, second edition. Oxford University Press.

Fish, Stanley E. 2012. *How to Write a Sentence: And How to Read One*. HarperCollins.

Fisher, Douglas, Nancy Frey, and John Hattie. 2016. *Visible Learning for Literacy: Implementing the Practices That Work Best to Accelerate Student Learning*. Corwin.

Foursha-Stevenson, Cass, Elena Nicoladis, René Trombley, Kurt Hablado, Derek Phung, and Kaley Dallaire. 2024. "Pronoun Comprehension and Cross-Linguistic Influence in Monolingual and Bilingual Children." *International Journal of Bilingualism* 28 (3): 479–493. doi. org/10.1177/13670069231170968.

Frey, Nancy, and Douglas Fisher. 2013. *Rigorous Reading: 5 Access Points for Comprehending Complex Texts*. Corwin.

Gallagher, Kelly. 2004. *Deeper Reading*. Stenhouse.

Gallagher, Kelly. 2011. *Write Like This: Teaching Real-World Writing Through Modeling and Mentor Texts*. Stenhouse.

Gallagher, Kelly, and Penny Kittle. 2018. "Giving Students the Right Kind of Writing Practice." *Educational Leadership* 75 (7): 14–20. ascd.org/el/articles/giving-students-the-right-kind-of-writing-practice.

Gaskell, Mike. 2021. "Now More Than Ever, Students Need 'Small Wins' to Put Big Goals in Reach." ASCD (blog), November 4, 2021. ascd.org/blogs/now-more-than-ever-students-need-small-wins-to-put-big-goals-in-reach.

Gentry, Richard, Jan McNeel, and Vickie Wallace-Nesler. 2014. *Fostering Writing in Today's Classroom*. Shell Education.

Graham, Steve, Alisha Bollinger, Carol Booth Olson, Catherine D'Aoust, Charles MacArthur, Deborah McCutchen, and Natalie Olinghouse. 2012. *Teaching Elementary School Students to Be Effective Writers: A Practice Guide* (NCEE 2012-4058). Washington, DC: National Center for Education Evaluation and Regional Assistance, Institute of Education Sciences, U.S. Department of Education. ies.ed.gov/ncee/wwc/Docs/practiceguide/writing_pg_062612.pdf.

Graham, Steve, and Michael A. Hebert. 2010. *Writing to Read: Evidence for How Writing Can Improve Reading*. A Carnegie Corporation Time to Act Report. Alliance for Excellent Education.

Graham, Steve, and Dolores Perin. 2007. *Writing Next: Effective Strategies to Improve Writing of Adolescents in Middle and High Schools*. carnegie.org/publications/writing-next-effective-strategies-to-improve-writing-of-adolescents-in-middle-and-high-schools.

Graves, Donald H. 1983. *Writing: Teachers & Children at Work*. Heinemann.

Graves, Donald H., and Penny Kittle. 2005. *Inside Writing: How to Teach the Details of Craft*. Heinemann.

Hattie, John, and Shirley Clarke. 2019. *Visible Learning: Feedback*. Routledge.

Johnson, Matthew. 2020. *Flash Feedback: Responding to Student Writing Better and Faster—Without Burning Out*. Corwin.

Jump, Jennifer, and Kathleen Kopp. 2023. *What the Science of Reading Says About Reading Comprehension and Content Knowledge*. Shell Education.

King, Jude. 2019. "The Big Power of Small Wins." *Medium*. June 7, 2019. medium.com/swlh/the-big-power-of-small-wins-c7709c9e10af.

King, Stephen. 2000. *On Writing: A Memoir of the Craft*. Scribner.

Kittle, Penny. 2008. *Write Beside Them: Risk, Voice, and Clarity in High School Writing*. Heinemann.

Kittle, Penny. 2022. *Micro Mentor Texts: Using Short Passages from Great Books to Teach Writer's Craft*. Scholastic.

Laminack, Lester L. 2016. *Cracking Open the Author's Craft: Teaching the Art of Writing*. Scholastic.

Lemov, Doug, Colleen Driggs, and Erica Woolway. 2016. *Reading Reconsidered: A Practical Guide to Rigorous Literacy Instruction*. Jossey-Bass.

Marzano, Robert J. 2009. "Helping Students Process Information." *Educational Leadership* 67 (2): 86–87.

McLeod, Saul. 2023. "Short-Term Memory in Psychology: Types, Duration and Capacity." SimplyPsychology, October 4, 2023. simplypsychology.org/short-term-memory.html.

Moats, Louisa Cook. 2020. *Speech to Print: Language Essentials for Teachers*, third edition. Paul H. Brookes.

Modern Language Association of America. 2020. "How Do I Use Singular They?" March 4, 2020. style.mla.org/using-singular-they.

Murray, Donald M. 1972. "Teach Writing as a Process Not Product." *The Leaflet* Fall 1972: 11–14.

National Commission on Writing. 2003. "The Neglected 'R': The Need for a Writing Revolution." College Entrance Examination Board. files.eric.ed.gov/fulltext/ED475856.pdf.

National Reading Panel (U.S.) and National Institute of Child Health and Human Development (U.S.). 2000. *Report of the National Reading Panel: Teaching Children to Read: An Evidence-based Assessment of the Scientific Research Literature on Reading and Its Implications for Reading Instruction*. U.S. Dept. of Health and Human Services, Public Health Service, National Institutes of Health, National Institute of Child Health and Human Development.

Oska, Sandra, Edgar Lerma, and Joel Topf. 2020. "A Picture Is Worth a Thousand Views: A Triple Crossover Trial of Visual Abstracts to Examine Their Impact on Research Dissemination." *Journal of Medical Internet Research* 22 (12): e22327. doi.org/10.2196/22327.

Plotinsky, Miriam. 2024. "The Power of Habit Stacking." ASCD (blog), September 24, 2024. ascd.org/blogs/the-power-of-habit-stacking.

Rasinski, Timothy, Nancy Padak, Joanna Newton, and Evangeline Newton. 2011. "The Latin-Greek Connection: Building Vocabulary Through Morphological Study." *The Reading Teacher* 65 (2): 133–141. doi.org/10.1002/trtr.01015.

Rasinski, Timothy, Nancy Padak, Rick M. Newton, and Evangeline Newton. 2020. *Building Vocabulary with Greek and Latin Roots*, second edition. Shell Education.

Ray, Katie Wood. 1999. *Wondrous Words: Writers and Writing in the Elementary Classroom*. National Council of Teachers of English.

# REFERENCES

Roberts, Kathryn L., Rebecca R. Norman, Nell K. Duke, Paul Morsink, Nicole M. Martin, and Jennifer A. Knight. 2013. "Diagrams, Timelines, and Tables—Oh, My! Fostering Graphical Literacy." *The Reading Teacher* 67 (1): 12–24. doi.org/10.1002/TRTR.1174.

Romano, Tom. 1987. *Clearing the Way: Working with Teenage Writers*. Heinemann.

Schmoker, Mike. 2018. *Focus: Elevating the Essentials to Radically Improve Student Learning,* second edition. ASCD.

Schrodt, Katie, Erin FitzPatrick, Bonnie A. Barksdale, Brandi Nunnery, and Michelle Medlin Hasty. 2021. "Teaching Writing with Mentor Texts in Kindergarten." *YC: Young Children* 76 (3): 44–53. jstor.org/stable/27095189.

Schrodt, Katie, Erin FitzPatrick, and Amy Elleman. 2020. "Becoming Brave Spellers." *The Reading Teacher* 74 (2): 208–214. doi.org/10.1002/trtr.1923.

Schrodt, Katie, Erin FitzPatrick, and Janna McClain. 2023. "Supporting Emergent Writing with Oral Storytelling Strategies." *Reading Teacher* 76 (4): 511–517. doi.org/10.1002/trtr.2170.

Schwartz, Barry. 2016. *The Paradox of Choice: Why More Is Less*. Ecco.

Sedita, Joan. 2022. *The Writing Rope: A Framework for Explicit Writing Instruction in All Subjects*. Paul H. Brookes.

Shanahan, Timothy. 2020a. "How Can We Take Advantage of Reading-Writing Relationships?" *Shanahan on Literacy* (blog), February 22, 2020. shanahanonliteracy.com/blog/how-can-we-take-advantage-of-reading-writing-relationships.

Shanahan, Timothy. 2020b. "Teaching with Complex Text: Haven't You Ever Heard of the ZPD?" *Shanahan on Literacy* (blog), August 22, 2020. shanahanonliteracy.com/blog/teaching-with-complex-text-havent-you-ever-heard-of-the-zpd.

Shanahan, Timothy. 2023. "Should We Match Texts to Students' Reading Levels?" Distinguished Scholar Address, Reading and Literacy SIG, American Educational Research Association, Chicago, IL. April 13, 2023. shanahanonliteracy.com/publications/should-we-match-texts-to-students-reading-levels.

Shanahan, Timothy, Douglas Fisher, and Nancy Frey. 2012. "The Challenge of Challenging Text." *Educational Leadership* 69 (6): 58–62.

Terada, Youki. 2021. "Why Students Should Write in All Subjects." *The Research Is In* (blog). Edutopia. January 7, 2021. edutopia.org/article/why-students-should-write-all-subjects.

Thompson, Clive. 2016. "The Surprising History of the Infographic." *Smithsonian Magazine,* July 2016. smithsonianmag.com/history/surprising-history-infographic-180959563.

TNTP. 2018. *The Opportunity Myth: What Students Can Show Us About How School Is Letting Them Down—And How to Fix It*. tntp.org/publication/the-opportunity-myth.

Toister, Nathan A. 2020. "Storyboarding as a Prewriting Activity for Second Language." TESOL Working Paper Series, 18: 126–138 Department of English and Applied Linguistics, Hawaii Pacific University. hpu.edu/research-publications/tesol-working-papers/2020/6_toister_storyboard.pdf.

U.S. Department of Education, Office of Educational Technology. 2023. *Artificial Intelligence and the Future of Teaching and Learning: Insights and Recommendations*. Washington, DC. tech.ed.gov/files/2023/05/ai-future-of-teaching-and-learning-report.pdf.

U.S. Department of Education, Institute of Education Sciences, National Center for Education Statistics. 2024. National Assessment of Educational Progress (NAEP), various years, 1984–2023 Long-Term Trend Reading Assessments. nationsreportcard.gov/ltt/reading/student-experiences/?age=13/.

VandeHei, Jim, Mike Allen, and Roy Schwartz. 2022. *Smart Brevity: The Power of Saying More with Less*. Workman Publishing.

Weissman, Jerry. 2022. "The Power of Pictures in Presentation Design." *Forbes*, February 25, 2022. forbes.com/sites/jerryweissman/2022/02/25/the-power-of-pictures-in-presentation-design.

Wright, Julie. 2020. "Build Your Stack: Short Texts, Big Engagement." National Council of Teachers of English. June 29, 2020. ncte.org/blog/2019/06/build-stack-short-texts-big-engagement.

Zinsser, William. 2001 [1976]. *On Writing Well*. Harper.

# INDEX

## A

AAAWWUBBIS (subordinating conjunctions), 81, 89, 93
Abrams, Gracie, 74
ACE (Answer-Cite-Explain) formula, 43
actionable feedback, 99
adjectives, 35, 36, 43–44, 85
anchor charts
    for analyzing author's craft, 19, 20, 112, 114, 116
    for caption writing, 39
    for cohesion connectors, 31, 93
    for essay structure, 51
    for one-word revision, 87, 115
    overview of, 63–64
    for 10% Off Revision strategy, 88–89, 113
    for Unstuck List strategy, 81, 82, 117
    in writer's notebooks, 65, 87
Angelou, Maya, 4
annotation, 17–18, 26–31, 92–93
argumentative writing, 7, 69–70
artificial intelligence (AI), 57–58
*Artificial Intelligence and the Future of Teaching and Learning* (U.S. Department of Education Office of Educational Technology), 57
assessment of learning
    artificial intelligence in, 57
    feedback in (*see* feedback)
    grading in, 57, 97, 103–5, 120
    lessons informed by, 98, 100
    one-sentence summaries as, 23
    quick writes as, 22, 100
    state testing in, 43, 51
    3-by-5 strategy in, 42
    walking and talking to students in, 66, 101–102, 103
ATE (Answer-Text-Explain) formula, 43
*Atomic Habits* (Clear), 1, 21
audiences, 56
audiobooks, 14
author's craft
    anchor charts for analyzing, 19, 20, 112, 114, 116
    cohesion connectors in, 29–31
    core reading strategy for analyzing, 19–20
    italics in, 32–33
    overview of, 15

## B

background knowledge, 14
*Bartleby, the Scrivener: A Story of Wall-Street* (Melville), 2
Be Bold strategy, 36–37
"Because I could not stop for Death" (Dickinson), 4
books, 9, 13, 94
bracketing, 88
brave spelling, 9, 54, 62
Brown, Emma, 92

## C

captions, 39–40
Castellanos Contreras, José Arturo, 26, 28, 34–35, 43–44, 67, 84, 108
"The Challenge of Challenging Text" (Shanahan, Fisher & Frey), 5
challenging texts, 5–6
characters, 18, 72, 92–93, 119
ChatGPT, 57
Check and Go strategy, 102–3
close reading, 4, 19–20, 32–35
cognitive load, 5, 8
cohesion connectors, 29–31, 92–94
color marking, 18, 26, 30, 31, 92–93
complex texts, 5–6
comprehension, reading, 14, 29, 34, 51–52
conjunctions
    acronyms for remembering, 81, 83, 89, 93
    in Be Bold strategy, 36, 37
    as cohesion connectors, 31
coordinating conjunctions (FANBOYS), 83, 89, 93
core reading strategies, 17–22
core writing strategies, 60–66
*Cracking Open the Author's Craft: Teaching the Art of Writing* (Laminack), 15
cross-curricular writing, 8, 39–40, 52, 75, 76–77
cubes, 41, 90–91, 121–122

## D

Declaration of Independence, 4
deleting, 86, 87, 88–89, 113
dependent clauses, 81
Dickinson, Emily, 4
diction, 74
dictionaries, 36
digital notebooks, 65
drafting, 52, 53–54, 56, 61, 79
drawing, 9, 78–80

## E

editing, 52, 55, 56, 58, 60, 61
    *See also* revising
emerging readers and writers (grades K–2)
    captions practice for, 40
    cohesion connectors for, 31
    Evidence Battle strategy for, 45
    Give Me Five strategy for, 24
    grammar practice for, 27, 33, 35, 68
    infographic creation by, 77
    one-word revision strategy for, 87
    overview of writing instruction for, 8–9
    Power Writes for, 62
    sequencing practice for, 94
    Social Media Thesis strategy for, 70
    storyboarding for, 80
    10% Off Revision strategy for, 89
engagement, 3, 7, 8
English language, 27, 32, 38
English language learners. *See* multilingual learners
errors, 54, 55, 56
    *See also* feedback
Essa, Huda, 32, 110
essays, 7, 47, 51, 60
"Ever American" (Essa), 32, 110
evidence, in texts, 43–45, 105, 123
Expand a Sentence strategy, 84–85
experienced readers and writers (grades 6–12)
    captions practice for, 40
    cohesion connectors for, 31, 94
    Evidence Battle strategy for, 45
    grammar practice for, 33, 35
    infographic creation by, 77

# INDEX

Potent Quotables strategy for, 47
Social Media Thesis strategy for, 70
Song (Re)writer strategy for, 75
storyboarding for, 80
10% Off Revision strategy for, 83, 89
3-by-5 strategy for, 42
Unstuck List strategy for, 83
express-lane editing, 60

## F

FANBOYS (coordinating conjunctions), 83, 89, 93
feedback
    artificial intelligence in, 57
    characteristics of effective, 6–7, 98–100
    grading in, 57, 97, 103–105, 120
    in micro writing, 61–62
    in Roll a Revision strategy, 90
    strategies for giving of, 101–105, 120
55-word stories, 72
first- and second-draft reading (reentering texts), 14, 17–18, 25–27, 44, 77
first reads, 14, 17–18, 23–24, 41, 121
*Flash Feedback* (Johnson), 6–7, 98
flash fiction, 72
*Focus* (Schmoker), 16, 98
formative assessment. *See* assessment of learning

## G

Gettysburg Address, 4
Give Me Five strategy, 23–24
Give One and Get One protocol, 42
goal-setting, 1–2
Gorman, Amanda, 47
grade-level texts, 5–6
grading, 57, 97, 103–5, 120
    *See also* assessment of learning; feedback
grammar
    grading of, 104, 105
    in one-sentence summaries, 23, 36, 37, 67–68
    pronouns in, 25–28, 31
    in revising and editing, 55, 56, 58, 61, 85, 89
    syntax in, 34–35, 67–68, 81, 84, 85, 89
    in Unstuck List strategy, 81, 83
graphics, 9, 39–40, 76–80, 94
Greek and Latin roots, 38
growth mindset, 9

## H

habits, 21
*Harrison Bergeron* (Vonnegut), 4
"Homework: Helpful or Harmful?" (short text), 69, 81, 111
*How to Write a Sentence: And How to Read One* (Stanley), 63

## I

illustrations, 9, 39–40, 78–80, 94
independent clauses, 34, 81
independent silent reading, 14
index cards, 42, 61
infographics, 76–77
informational texts, 39–41, 69–70, 76–77, 80
italics, 32–33

## J

journals, 51
    *See also* writer's notebooks
*Julius Caesar* (Shakespeare), 13–14

## K

key details, 42
Key, Francis Scott, 73

## L

labels, 9, 62
Latin and Greek roots, 38
layered annotations strategies, 25–31
layered reading, 14, 17–18
lesson planners, 118
*Let it Happen* (Abrams), 74

## M

main idea, 23–24, 69–70, 76, 77
main points, 42
Mandl, György, 28, 34–35, 67, 108
marking up texts, 17–18, 26–31, 92–93
Melville, Herman, 2
memoirs, 71–72
memory, 5
mentor texts, 9, 63
micro-fiction, 72
micro writing, 60–62
mistakes, 54, 55, 56
    *See also* feedback
*Moby Dick* (Melville), 2
modeling, 9, 14, 17, 18, 25–26, 29–30
Modern Language Association (MLA), 27
motivation, 7, 8, 99–100
multilingual learners

cohesion connectors for, 31
Give Me Five strategy for, 24
grammar practice for, 27, 37, 68, 83, 85
one-word revision strategy for, 87
Potent Quotables strategy for, 47
storyboarding for, 78
3-by-5 strategy for, 42
"The Mystery of the Beeswax Wreck" (short text), 29–30, 109

## N

names, 25, 26, 27
nonfiction texts, 39–41, 69–70, 76–77, 80
"No Talking, No Walking" time, 22
notebooks, 64–65, 81, 87
    *See also* journals
*Not Quite What I Was Planning* (Smith & Fershleiser), 71
number cubes, 41, 90–91, 121–122

## O

objects, of sentences, 67
one-sentence summaries, 23, 36, 37, 67–68, 84–85
one-word revision, 86–87, 115
*On Writing* (King), 59
*On Writing Well* (Zinsser), 88
opinion writing, 7, 69–70
oral storytelling and rehearsal, 9
over-response, 98

## P

Pair and Share strategy, 102
paired reading, 14
*The Paradox of Choice* (Schwartz), 43
paragraphs, 29–31, 92, 93, 94
people, discussed in short texts, 18, 25–28, 72, 92–93, 119
persuasive writing, 7, 69–70
"Phenomenal Woman" (Angelou), 4
photographs, 39–40, 62, 65
phrases, 29–31, 34–35
picture books, 9, 94
    *See also* graphics
Pile and Grade strategy, 103–104
positive self-talk, 9
posters. *See* anchor charts
Potent Quotables strategy, 46–47
Power Writes, 62
Preamble to the Constitution, 4
predicates, 34, 67, 68
prewriting, 52, 53, 56, 58, 60, 78–80
printable rubrics, 120

© Shell Education

136447—Short Texts, Big Impact **131**

# INDEX

process writing, 52–57, 60–62
progress, 7, 99–100
prompts, 22, 44, 47, 69–70, 119
pronouns, 25–28, 31
publishing, 52, 53, 56, 57, 61–62
punctuation, 32–33, 55, 61, 71, 81, 105

## Q

questions
 on captions, 39
 on cohesion connectors, 31
 in Evidence Battle strategy, 43, 44, 45
 for first reads, 17–18, 41, 121
 on infographics, 76, 77
 in one-word revision strategy, 87
 for Song (Re)writer strategy, 74
 student creation of, 42
 when zooming in, 19–20, 32–33, 34, 35
quick writes, 21–22, 81, 100, 120
quotes, 46–47

## R

ratiocination, 92
read alouds, 14
reading
 Be Bold strategy for, 36–37
 Caption Creator strategy for, 39–40
 core strategies for, 17–22
 Evidence Battle strategy for, 43–45
 Give Me Five strategy for, 23–24
 layered annotations strategies for, 25–31
 overview of short text usage in, 2–8, 13–15
 Potent Quotables strategy for, 46–47
 Roll a Response strategy for, 41
 3-by-5 strategy for, 42
 tips for strategy usage in, 10
 Word Spokes strategy for, 38
 zooming in strategies for, 19–20, 32–35
reading comprehension, 14, 29, 34, 51–52
recursive writing process, 52–57, 60–62
reentering texts, 14, 17–18, 25–27, 44, 77
referential relationships, 26
refinement, 61
revising
 artificial intelligence in, 57, 58
 cohesion connectors in, 92–94
 in Expand a Sentence strategy, 84–85
 feedback in (*see* feedback)
 in micro writing, 60, 61
 in one-word revision strategy, 86–87, 115
 in recursive writing process, 52, 54–55, 56

in Roll a Revision strategy, 90–91
 with sticky notes, 66
 in storyboarding, 79
 in 10% Off Revision strategy, 83, 88–89, 113
 tips for strategy usage in, 10
Roll a Response strategy, 41, 121
Roll a Revision strategy, 90–91, 122
rubrics, 103–105, 120

## S

SCAMPER strategy, 86–87, 115
scoring, 57, 97, 103–105, 120
 *See also* assessment of learning; feedback
seating charts, 66, 101–2
second draft reading (reentering texts), 14, 17–18, 25–27, 44, 77
self-talk, 9
sentences
 cohesion connectors for, 29–30, 92–94
 expanding of, 84–85
 grading of, 105
 in mentor texts, 63
 as mini compositions, 2
 in one- and two-sentence summaries, 23, 36, 37, 67–68
 in one-word revision strategy, 86–87
 punctuation in, 32–33
 in six-word memoirs, 71
 syntax in, 34–35, 67–68, 81, 84, 85, 89
 in 10% Off Revision strategy, 89
 for thesis statements, 69–70
 Unstuck List strategy for, 81–83
sentence strips, 69, 70, 71
sequencing, 94
Shakespeare, William, 13–14
shared writing experiences, 9, 68, 70, 77
sharing and comparing of writing
 in argumentative writing, 69–70
 caption writing in, 39
 in drafting process, 53
 infographics in, 77
 one- and two-sentence summaries for, 36, 37, 67
 in one-word revision strategy, 87
 in Pair and Share strategy, 102
 quick writes for, 22
 in Roll a Response strategy, 41
 in Roll a Revision strategy, 90
 six-word memoirs for, 71, 72
 in storyboarding, 79
 in 3-by-5 strategy, 42
 in Unstuck List strategy, 82
 *See also* publishing

short drafting, 61
short prewriting, 60
Short Rubric strategy, 103–104
short text lesson planners, 118
short texts
 benefits of using, 2–8
 reading strategies for (*see* reading)
 tips on strategy usage for, 10
 writing and revising strategies for (*see* revising; writing)
silent independent reading, 14
six-word memoirs, 71–72
sketching, 9, 78–80
*Small but Mighty: How Everyday Habits Add Up to More Manageable and Confident Teaching* (Plotinsky), 21
small publishing, 61–62
small revision and editing, 61
small wins, 7, 99
*Smart Brevity* (VandeHei, Allen & Schwartz), 4
social-emotional learning (SEL), 8
*Social-Emotional Learning Starts with Us* (DiFazio), 8
Social Media Thesis strategy, 69–70
Song (Re)writer strategy, 73–75
specific feedback, 98
spelling, 9, 54, 62
stamps and stickers, 66, 102–103
"The Star-Spangled Banner" (Key), 73
state standards, 41, 43, 91
state writing assessments, 43, 51
Stealers Wheel, 81
sticky notes
 in Evidence Battle strategy, 44
 in grading, 103–4, 105
 in micro writing, 61
 in quick writes, 22
 in revising, 66
 in Roll a Response strategy, 41
 in storyboarding, 79, 80
 in three-word summary sentences, 67
 in Unstuck List strategy, 82
Sticky Note Revision strategy, 66
storyboarding, 78–80, 124
storytelling, 9, 71–72
strategic stopping points, 21
strategies
 for giving feedback (*see* feedback)
 for reading with short texts (*see* reading)
 tips on usage of, 10
 for writing and revising short texts (*see* revising; writing)
struggling readers, 5–6, 8

**132** 136447—Short Texts, Big Impact

© Shell Education

# INDEX

student engagement and motivation, 3, 7, 8

subjects, of sentences, 34, 67, 68

subordinating conjunctions (AAAWWUBBIS), 81, 89, 93

Sullivan, Mr. (teacher), 2, 46

summaries
- in Be Bold strategy, 36, 37
- in Expand a Sentence strategy, 84–85
- in Give Me Five strategy, 23
- in six-word memoirs, 72
- in 3-by-5 strategy, 42
- in three-word summary sentences, 67–68

Swift, Taylor, 73

synonyms, 73–74

syntax, 34–35, 67–68, 81, 84, 85, 89

## T

techniques, in author's craft. *See* author's craft

10% Off Revision strategy, 83, 88–89, 113

text-dependent writing prompts, 44, 119

text evidence, 43–45, 105, 123

texts. *See* short texts

thesis statements, 69–70

"they" pronoun, 27

thinking aloud, 9, 17

"This or That" activity, 45

Thoreau, Henry David, 46

3-by-5 strategy, 42

three-word summary sentences, 67–68, 84–85

timely feedback, 6–7, 98

timers, 42, 44, 61

tone, 74

Two-Minute Rule, 21

two-sentence summaries, 37

Two-Word Sentence Smack Down, 67

## U

Unstuck List, 81–83, 117

## V

verbs, 34, 36, 37, 67, 68

visual texts, 39–40, 76–77

vocabulary, 14, 36–38

Vonnegut, Kurt, 4

## W

*Walden* (Thoreau), 46

walking and talking to students, 66, 101–2, 103

Washington, George, 4

"What's Right at All Costs" (Scott), 25, 26, 28, 34–35, 43–44, 84, 108

*What the Science Says About Reading Comprehension and Content Knowledge* (Jump & Kopp), 34

Wiesel, Elie, 47

Word Spokes strategy, 38

word walls, 24

working memory, 5

work motivation, 7, 8, 99–100

writer's notebooks, 64–65, 81, 87
- *See also* journals

writing
- assessment of (*see* assessment of learning; feedback)
- author's craft in, 15, 19–20
- of captions, 39–40
- cohesion connectors in, 92–94
- core strategies for, 60–66
- evidence from texts in, 45, 105, 123
- famous quotations in, 47
- goal-setting in, 1–2
- of infographics, 76–77
- overview of short text usage in, 3–9, 51–58
- in quick writes, 21–22
- revising of (*see* revising)
- sharing and comparing of (*see* sharing and comparing of writing)
- of six-word memoirs, 71–72
- Social Media Thesis strategy for, 69–70
- Song (Re)writer strategy for, 73–75
- storyboarding for, 78–80, 124
- of summaries (*see* summaries)
- tips for strategy usage in, 10
- Unstuck List strategy for, 81–83, 117

writing checklists, 9

*Writing Next* (Graham & Perin), 52, 63

writing process, 52–57, 60–62

writing prompts, 22, 44, 47, 69–70, 119

*The Writing Rope* (Sedita), 84

*Writing: Teachers & Children at Work* (Graves), 52, 54

*Writing to Read* (Graham & Hebert), 52

## Y

yarn toss activity, 31

young children. *See* emerging readers and writers (grades K–2)

*Your Fantastic Elastic Brain* (Deak), 9

Yousafzai, Malala, 47

## Z

zooming in strategies, 19–20, 32–35

# ABOUT THE AUTHOR

**Kim Carlton, M.Ed.,** is a dedicated educator, writer, and advocate for the transformative power of literacy. With over two decades of experience teaching and mentoring, she has encouraged many students and educators to develop a love for reading and writing. Her extensive career includes roles as a classroom teacher of English and creative writing, an instructional specialist coaching and training teachers, a district literacy specialist supporting writers at all levels, and a director of secondary language arts at a large, diverse school district. Kim has also taught preservice educators and led summer writing institutes for teachers.

Kim holds a master's degree in educational administration from East Texas A&M University. She taught at Richardson Independent School District (Texas), where she was honored as Secondary Teacher of the Year. As a contributing author to *What the Science of Reading Says About Writing* (Shell Education), Kim combined research-driven insights with her heartfelt mission to empower writers everywhere.

Today, Kim provides professional development to teachers worldwide, but her favorite moments are spent side-by-side with novice writers discovering for the first time that writing isn't as hard as they imagined. Based in Dallas, Kim shares her life with her endlessly patient husband and two less-than-patient rescue dogs.

# DIGITAL RESOURCES

## Accessing the Digital Resources

The digital resources can be downloaded by following these steps:

1. Go to **www.tcmpub.com/digital**
2. Use the ISBN number to redeem the digital resources.
3. Respond to the question using the book.
4. Follow the prompts on the Content Cloud website to sign in or create a new account.
5. The content redeemed will now be on your My Content screen. Click on the product to look through the digital resources. All resources are available for download. Select files can be previewed, opened, and shared.

For questions and assistance with your ISBN redemption, please contact Teacher Created Materials.

**email:** customerservice@tcmpub.com

**phone:** 800-858-7339

## Contents of the Digital Resources

The Digital Resources include digital versions of all of the student pages and forms in this book.